DREAM PILGRIMS

A JOURNEY INTO THE SUBCONSCIOUS

RANJEET SINGH

This book is lovingly dedicated to my friends, colleagues, and family members — the dreamers who have generously opened the windows to their subconscious, sharing their most intimate night-time visions with me.

Each dream you shared was a thread in the rich tapestry of this study, leading me deeper into the realm of the subconscious. Your vivid recounts, curious symbols, and heartfelt interpretations have enriched my understanding and been the guiding stars in my journey through the world of dreams.

To my colleagues, who have walked with me on this journey of discovery, offering insights and challenging notions and broadening the horizons of my knowledge, your intellectual companionship has been invaluable.

To my friends, who have been the sounding boards for my wildest theories and the most patient listeners to my incessant musings about the world of dreams — your support and encouragement have been the bedrock of this endeavour.

And to my family, who have always believed in the power of dreams and supported my fascination with them — your love and belief in my work have been the strongest motivators.

This book is a tribute to all of you, a celebration of the dreams that connect us, and a testament to the endless possibilities that they represent. Thank you for embarking on this journey with me and making my dream come true.

With heartfelt gratitude and love,

Ranjeet Singh

Contents

Preface

Welcome to "Dream Pilgrims - A Journey into the Subconscious," a book that invites you on an explorative journey into the enigmatic and profound world of dreams. Dreams have always been a source of mystery and fascination, a bridge between the waking world and the depths of our subconscious mind. In this book, we embark on a pilgrimage, not to a physical destination, but into our dreamscapes' rich and often uncharted territory.

This book is a culmination of my lifelong fascination with dreams, a journey that began in the quiet corners of my childhood, where night-time visions and daydreams blurred the lines of reality and imagination. Over the years, as I delved deeper into the study of dreams, I discovered a universal thread - dreams are a shared human experience, yet deeply personal in their language and symbolism.

"Dream Pilgrims" explores various cultural, psychological, and spiritual perspectives on dreaming. It draws from a wide range of sources, including ancient texts, modern psychological theories, and personal anecdotes, weaving together a tapestry that illustrates the multifaceted nature of dreams.

Each chapter in this book is designed to guide you through different aspects of dreaming - from historical theories and cultural interpretations to dreams' spiritual and therapeutic dimensions. We will explore how dreams are perceived in different cultures, how they have been understood throughout history, and how modern science contributes to our current understanding of this mysterious phenomenon.

But more than just an exploration of theories, "Dream Pilgrims" invites you, the reader, to engage with your dreams. It encourages you to become a pilgrim in your own right, exploring the landscapes of your subconscious mind and discovering the personal significance and wisdom your dreams hold.

Whether you are a curious explorer of the night's tales, a student of psychology, a seeker of spiritual truths, or someone looking for a deeper understanding of your inner world, this book is for you. I hope that "Dream Pilgrims" will intrigue you and inspire you to embark on your journey of self-discovery through the world of dreams.

So, let us begin this journey with open minds and a sense of wonder as we step into the fascinating realm of the subconscious.

With warm regards,
Ranjeet Singh

CHAPTER ONE

The Fascination with Dreams

Have you ever woken up from a dream so vivid, so engulfing, that you felt it was a part of your waking life? Maybe it was a dream where you flew across the skies, or perhaps one where a departed loved one whispered words of wisdom. These nightly visitors' dreams have always been mysterious and fascinating. They are like a secret door to an inner world, a world that each of us, including you, possesses yet often understands so little about.

Think about the last dream you remember. What did you feel? Was it joy, fear, or confusion? Dreams can evoke emotions that sometimes feel more intense than our day-to-day experiences. They can be a mirror, reflecting our deepest desires, fears, and even untold stories. But have you ever wondered why we dream what we dream? Why does your mind paint such elaborate, sometimes bizarre, pictures while you sleep?

Common understanding suggests dreams are just random firings of a resting brain. But is that all they are? Just a meaningless rerun of daily events or a jumbled collection of memories? Perhaps there's more, especially when you think about dreams that seemed to have predicted a future event or offered a solution to your problem. How often have we heard stories of great inventors or artists who found their inspiration in a dream?

As we delve deeper into this exploration, let's consider some common dream scenarios that many, including yourself, might have experienced. Have you ever been in a dream, walking through a dark, dense jungle? The air is thick with an eerie silence, and your heart pounds as you navigate the undergrowth. Suddenly, you're surrounded by snakes slithering around your feet, their hisses breaking the silence. You want to run, but your feet are rooted to the spot. This dream, frightening as it may be, is laden with symbolism and hidden meanings. In many cultures, snakes are seen as symbols of transformation or fear. What could this dream be telling you? Is it about confronting your fears, or is it signalling a transformation, perhaps one you're not yet aware of?

Or consider the all-too-common dream of falling. You're walking along a path, and suddenly, the ground gives way beneath you. You're plummeting into an abyss, your heart in your throat, adrenaline coursing through your veins. This sensation of falling is one of the most primal dream experiences. Often, it is interpreted as a manifestation of losing control or anxiety about a situation in your waking life. But what if it's more than that? What if it's a call to let go of something no longer serving you?

And then there are those dreams where you're trying to speak or shout, but no sound comes out. You're voiceless in a situation that desperately demands your voice. This could reflect feelings of powerlessness or frustration in your waking life. Maybe it's a sign that you feel unheard in certain areas of your life or struggle to express yourself.

These dreams, and countless others like them, are not just random concoctions of the sleeping brain. They carry messages, lessons, and insights. This book will explore these common dream scenarios and how different cultures, especially the rich Indian tradition, interpret these dreams.

In Indian philosophy, dreams are often viewed as significant indicators of one's inner state and can even be seen as prophetic. The ancient texts of Hinduism, like the Upanishads, delve deeply into the concept of dreams, offering profound and practical insights. As we journey through this book, we will explore these ancient teachings and see how they can apply to our modern understanding of dreams.

As you embark on this journey through the pages of this book, I invite you to open your mind to the possibility that dreams could be a language of their own. A language that, once deciphered, could offer insights into your deepest self. This book isn't just about understanding dreams from a global perspective; it's about exploring the labyrinth of your subconscious, where every dream has a story to tell, a lesson to impart.

In the following chapters, we'll dive into the world of dreams, drawing from the rich tapestry of Indian culture and Hindu philosophy and insights from around the globe. You'll learn about the types of dreams, the symbolism that pervades your nighttime narratives, and the fascinating link between dreams and your emotional world.

So, as you turn each page, keep an open mind and heart. Reflect on your dreams, the strange, the scary, the mystifying. Each one is a piece of the puzzle that is your inner self. Together, we will explore these dreamscapes, understand their symbolism, and perhaps even learn to speak the language of our subconscious. Let's continue this journey into the fascinating world of dreams, where every night is an adventure into the unknown.

Importance in Indian Culture

In the rich tapestry of Indian culture, dreams hold a place of profound significance. They are not merely nocturnal narratives; they are viewed as vital links between the conscious mind and the deeper, more mystical realms of existence.

Dreams in Indian culture are often seen as more than just subconscious reflections; they are sometimes considered messages from the divine, omens of the future, or insights into one's true self. The ancient scriptures of Hinduism, such as the Vedas and Upanishads, are replete with references to dreams, indicating their esteemed place in the Indian psyche. Dreams are not just personal experiences; they are believed to be connected with the universe's universal truths and cosmic play.

In Hindu philosophy, the concept of 'Maya' or illusion is central. Dreams are often interpreted within this framework, considered both real and unreal, existing in a liminal space that bridges our daily life and the higher truths of existence. This duality of dreams – illusory and insightful – makes them an intriguing subject in Indian thought.

Moreover, Indian culture recognizes the potential of dreams in personal growth and spiritual enlightenment. Great sages and seers of India have often spoken about the significance of dream interpretation to achieve higher consciousness and self-realization. Dreams are seen as a medium through which one can gain a deeper understanding of the self and the workings of the mind.

In therapeutic practices, particularly those influenced by Indian traditions like Ayurveda and yoga, dreams are used as tools for healing and self-exploration. They reflect one's physical, emotional, and spiritual health, providing clues to imbalances and insights into healing.

But dreams are valued not just in the spiritual or therapeutic realms. In the everyday life of Indian society, dreams find their place in customs, folklore, and daily conversations. Based on ancient texts and cultural beliefs, dream interpretations often guide important decisions and life events.

Expanding further into Indian culture and its relationship with dreams, we find that Hindu texts offer a wealth of knowledge and perspectives. These ancient scriptures discuss dreams and provide insightful examples, demonstrating their significance in the spiritual and philosophical fabric of Indian life.

One of the most notable references to dreams in Hindu scripture is the Brihadaranyaka Upanishad, one of the oldest Upanishads. It presents a detailed discourse on the nature of dreams. According to this text, dreams are not mere illusions but a realm where the soul (Atman) is free from the constraints of the physical world. The Upanishad elaborates on how, in dreams, the soul departs from the body and travels in the dream world, experiencing different realities that could offer profound spiritual insights.

Another critical text, the Mandukya Upanishad, delves into the states of consciousness. It classifies dreams as a distinct state of consciousness, different from waking and deep sleep. In this state, known as the 'Swapna,' the individual becomes the creator, experiencing a world entirely of their own making. This concept underscores dreams' creative and subjective nature, offering a rich ground for introspection and self-discovery.

The Mahabharata, one of the great epics of Hindu literature, contains numerous instances where dreams are pivotal to the narrative. For example, King Dhritarashtra's dream of a jackal howling in his palace, interpreted by Vidura, foretells the downfall of his kingdom. This story not only illustrates the prophetic nature of dreams in Indian culture but also highlights the importance of dream interpretation.

In the Ramayana, another epic, dreams serve as omens and divine messages. King Dasharatha, the father of Lord Rama, dreams of his ancestors warning him about impending misfortune, a dream that foreshadows the following epic events. These examples from the epics demonstrate how dreams are woven into the fabric of Indian storytelling and mythology, reflecting their deep cultural and spiritual significance.

In addition to these texts, Indian folklore and traditional practices are replete with references to dreams. Dreams are often considered integral to one's spiritual journey, offering guidance, warnings, and insights. Astrologers and priests, even in contemporary times, often interpret dreams to provide counsel and direction in personal and communal matters.

This chapter, therefore, is not just an exploration of the importance of dreams in Indian culture; it's an invitation to delve into a rich historical and spiritual tradition that has revered and sought meaning in the world of dreams for millennia. As we journey through these ancient texts and stories, we uncover a deep-seated belief that dreams are a bridge between the mortal and the divine, the known and the unknown, offering a unique lens through which one can view and understand the deeper truths of life.

CHAPTER THREE

The Science of Dreaming

Let's look into the fascinating world of the science behind dreaming, unravelling the mysteries in our brains each night. Understanding dreams' biological and psychological mechanisms satiate our curiosity and provide a foundation for interpreting their significance in our lives.

The Brain at Night: Unraveling the Mysteries
Our brain doesn't simply shut down when we drift off to sleep. Instead, it embarks on a complex and dynamic journey. Various stages of sleep, including Rapid Eye Movement (REM) and Non-REM sleep, play host to different types of dreams. REM sleep, characterized by rapid movements of the eyes, is the stage most commonly associated with vivid dreaming. During this phase, the brain is almost as active as it is when we are awake, but what makes it intriguing is the change in the pattern of brain activity. Research has shown that during REM sleep, the prefrontal cortex, responsible for logical thinking and decision-making, becomes less active. In contrast, the limbic system, which governs emotions, becomes more active. This shift might explain why dreams can be

emotionally intense and often defy logical structures.

The Role of Neurotransmitters

Neurotransmitters, the brain's chemical messengers, play a crucial role in sleep and dreaming. Serotonin and norepinephrine, known for regulating mood and arousal, drop significantly during REM sleep. This reduction is thought to contribute to the heightened emotional content of dreams. Meanwhile, acetylcholine, another neurotransmitter, remains high, which may contribute to dreams' vividness and sometimes erratic nature.

The Function of Dreams

But why do we dream? This question has puzzled scientists and philosophers for centuries. One theory, the Activation-Synthesis Hypothesis, suggests that dreams result from the brain's attempt to make sense of random neural activity during sleep. Another compelling theory is the Threat Simulation Theory, which proposes that dreaming serves an evolutionary purpose, allowing us to rehearse responses to threats in a safe environment. More recent research points towards dreams being crucial for emotional regulation and memory consolidation. Dreams, particularly during REM sleep, help us process and make sense of our emotional experiences from the day. They may serve as a cognitive space where we can safely confront and work through emotions and memories, contributing to our mental health and well-being.

Dreams and Memory

There's also a fascinating link between dreams and memory. Some studies suggest that dreaming helps consolidate memories, transferring information from short-term to long-term memory storage. This process could be crucial for learning and retaining new information.

Dreams and the Subconscious Mind

Another compelling aspect of dreaming involves the subconscious mind. While our conscious mind takes a backseat during sleep, the subconscious becomes more prominent. This transition could explain why dreams often tap into memories, fears, and desires we are unaware of during our waking hours. The subconscious mind speaks in the language of symbols and emotions, which might explain our dreams' often surreal and symbolic nature.

The REM and Non-REM Dream States

While REM sleep is most commonly associated with vivid dreaming, it's not the only dream stage. Dreams also occur during non-REM sleep, though they are usually less intense and more thought-like. The difference in dreaming between these stages could be linked to variations in brain activity. Non-REM dreams are thought to result from the brain processing and integrating emotional experiences, while REM dreams are more about integrating these experiences with existing memories.

Sleep Disorders and Dreams

The study of sleep disorders has also shed light on the science of dreaming. Conditions like insomnia, sleep apnea, and narcolepsy not only disrupt sleep patterns but can also have a significant impact on dreaming. For instance, people with narcolepsy often enter REM sleep rapidly and may experience vivid, often disturbing dreams. Understanding these disorders helps us appreciate the delicate balance required for healthy sleep and, by extension, healthy dreaming.

Lucid Dreaming: Awareness Within the Dream

Lucid dreaming offers another fascinating perspective, where the dreamer becomes aware that they are dreaming. This phenomenon blurs the lines between consciousness and unconsciousness and has been the subject of much scientific investigation. Studies on lucid dreaming have revealed that it involves a unique state of consciousness, where the dreamer can often control aspects of the dream. It's believed that this occurs due to a reactivation of brain parts involved in self-awareness and executive functions during REM sleep.

The Future of Dream Research

Our understanding of dreams is rapidly evolving with technological advancements, such as neuroimaging and machine learning. Scientists are now beginning to decode dream content, offering unprecedented insights into how our brains create and process dreams. This research not only promises to deepen our understanding of sleep and dreaming but also has potential implications for mental health treatment, offering new pathways to address issues like PTSD and depression.

Integrating Science with Experience

As we traverse the scientific landscape of dreams, it becomes clear that these nightly escapades are a complex interplay of biology, psychology, and personal experience. The science of dreaming helps demystify some aspects of this experience and opens the door to new questions and mysteries. In the next chapters, we'll explore how this scientific understanding intertwines with cultural interpretations and personal experiences, creating a comprehensive picture of the world of dreams.

As we delve deeper into the science of dreaming, we appreciate the complex interplay between our brains and dreams. Understanding this intricate dance can offer insights into the nature of our dreams and what they might signify. The following chapters will explore how these scientific insights intersect with cultural and philosophical interpretations of dreams, providing a more holistic understanding of our nighttime journeys.

CHAPTER FOUR

Types of Dreams

Imagine embarking on a nightly odyssey, a journey where each dream is a unique path woven into the fabric of your subconscious. These paths are as varied and mysterious as the landscapes of our minds, each type of dream offering a different experience, a different revelation. As we venture into the realm of dreams, prepare ourselves for an exploration that is not just about understanding but also about discovering the enigmatic and often hidden aspects of your psyche. From the enigmatic whispers of symbolic dreams to the heart-racing intensity of nightmares, each dream category holds secrets waiting to be unveiled. Are you ready to uncover these mysteries? Let's cautiously tread into this diverse world of dreams, where each turn could reveal startling insights, and each shadow could hold profound meanings. With a mix of anticipation and curiosity, let's unravel the intricate types of dreams that visit us in the quiet of the night.

1. Lucid Dreams: Awareness in Dreaming
Lucid dreams are a fascinating and exhilarating aspect of our dream experiences, where you become aware that you're dreaming. Picture yourself in an unusual scenario, like walking through a market with backwards-moving

clock hands and suddenly realizing it's all a dream. This awareness can range from a mere acknowledgement to the ability to control the dream's environment and narrative. The intensity of lucid dreams varies, with some dreamers able to deliberately manipulate their surroundings, while others may simply be conscious observers. Beyond mere enjoyment, lucid dreaming can have therapeutic benefits, particularly for those dealing with nightmares, as it offers a way to confront and reshape distressing dreams. It's also a rich ground for creativity and problem-solving, unbound by real-world limitations.

Techniques such as maintaining a dream journal, performing reality checks, and specific meditation practices are often employed to induce lucid dreams. Some even use methods like the Wake Back to Bed (WBTB), which involves waking up after several hours of sleep and returning to sleep to enter a lucid dream. However, it's important to approach lucid dreaming with caution to avoid sleep disturbances, and those with certain mental health conditions should consult a professional beforehand. In essence, lucid dreams blend the boundaries of consciousness and offer a unique realm where imagination is the only limit, making them a significant and intriguing part of our dreaming life.

2. Nightmares: Facing Our Fears

Nightmares are a powerful and often distressing type of dream, typically involving scenarios that evoke fear, anxiety, or despair. These dreams are more than mere unsettling images; they are vivid, emotionally intense experiences that can leave a lasting impact even after waking. Imagine being chased by an unseen threat in a dark, endless forest or finding yourself in imminent danger.

Such scenarios in nightmares often mirror our innermost fears and anxieties, bringing to the surface issues we might struggle with in our waking lives. They can reflect stress, trauma, or even day-to-day worries. While nightmares can be unsettling, they also serve a purpose in our emotional and psychological processing. By confronting the content of nightmares, either independently or with professional guidance, we can gain insights into unresolved issues and find ways to address underlying fears or stressors. Nightmares, while challenging, can be a significant tool for self-reflection and emotional growth, urging us to face and understand the deeper aspects of our psyche.

3. Recurring Dreams: Echoes of the Mind

Recurring dreams, those persistent narratives that visit us night after night, are like echoes of the mind, revealing deeper patterns and unresolved issues in our subconscious. These dreams often have a consistent theme or setting, such as being lost in an unknown place, failing an exam, or missing an important event. Their repetitive nature is not merely a coincidence; it signifies something significant that your mind is trying to process or resolve. For example, repeatedly dreaming about being unable to find your way back home might symbolize a deeper search for stability or identity in your life. The frequency and intensity of these dreams can vary, but their persistence usually points towards an emotional or psychological aspect that requires attention. Recurring dreams can act as a mirror, reflecting our fears, anxieties, unresolved conflicts, or even unfulfilled desires. By recognizing the patterns in these dreams and understanding their symbolism, we can gain valuable insights into our inner world. This understanding can lead to a resolution of the underlying issues, often causing the recurring dreams to diminish or cease. Recurring dreams are a powerful tool for introspection and self-awareness, urging us to look deeper into our thoughts, feelings, and experiences to find harmony and understanding.

4. Prophetic Dreams: Glimpses of the Future

Prophetic dreams, also known as precognitive dreams, hold a special allure as they seem to offer glimpses into the future. These are the dreams where you experience events or see images that astonishingly relate to something that occurs later in real life. Imagine dreaming about a friend you haven't thought about in years, only to receive a call from them the next day. Or consider a dream where you see a specific place in vivid detail, a place you've never been, only to find yourself there unexpectedly weeks or months later. These experiences can be both mystifying and intriguing, blurring the lines between the subconscious mind and the realm of future possibilities. While the scientific community remains sceptical about the existence of true prophetic dreams, numerous anecdotal accounts and cultural narratives around them suggest a different story. In many cultures, such dreams are considered significant and often seen as messages or warnings. Whether these dreams are a manifestation of our intuitive understanding or a true foresight into future events, they continue to be a subject of fascination and wonder. Prophetic dreams challenge our understanding of time and consciousness, inviting us to explore the more mysterious and unexplained aspects of our dream experiences.

5. Healing Dreams: Messages for Well-being

Healing dreams are profound and therapeutic dreams,

often providing insight, guidance, or even solutions related to our well-being. These dreams can manifest as messages about health, emotional healing, or spiritual growth. Imagine, for instance, dreaming about walking in a lush, green forest, feeling a sense of deep peace and rejuvenation. Upon waking, you might find that this dream has alleviated some of your stress or anxiety, offering a sense of renewal. In another scenario, you might dream of a deceased loved one offering advice or comfort, which can be a powerful source of healing, especially during times of grief or emotional distress. Healing dreams can also be more literal, perhaps alerting you to health issues. There have been instances where individuals have dreamt of ailments or bodily discomforts, which later prompted medical check-ups, revealing underlying health conditions. These dreams tap into the intuitive knowledge of our bodies and minds, often providing clarity and understanding that we might not be consciously aware of. They can be instrumental in guiding us towards better caring for our physical, emotional, and spiritual health. In essence, healing dreams are a nurturing and insightful aspect of our subconscious, offering messages of restoration and balance.

6. Symbolic Dreams: The Language of the Subconscious
Symbolic dreams are a captivating and intricate aspect of our dream world, often speaking the profound language of the subconscious through metaphors and imagery. In these dreams, each element carries a deeper meaning, often unique to the individual's experiences and psyche. For instance, imagine dreaming about flying – a common symbolic dream. This could represent a desire for freedom, liberation from constraints, or an aspiration to reach new heights. Alternatively, consider a dream where you're

navigating a maze. This could symbolize the complexities and challenges you're facing in your waking life, reflecting feelings of confusion or the search for a solution. Symbolic dreams often require introspection and personal interpretation, as the same symbol can mean different things to different people. A body of water, for example, might represent emotional depth for one person, while for another, it might symbolize a barrier or an unknown journey. These dreams tap into our innermost thoughts, fears, desires, and questions, providing insights into our inner world. By reflecting on and interpreting the symbols in these dreams, we can uncover hidden aspects of ourselves and gain a deeper understanding of our emotions, conflicts, and life paths. Symbolic dreams, therefore, are not just a phenomenon of our sleeping minds but a powerful tool for self-discovery and personal growth.

7. Vivid Dreams: Intense and Memorable

Vivid dreams are those intensely realistic and memorable dreams that stay with us long after awakening. These dreams are characterized by their striking clarity, rich detail, and powerful emotions. Imagine a dream where you're walking through a vibrant market – the colours are brighter than anything you've seen, the sounds are clear, and you can even feel the texture of objects you touch. Such vividness can make the dream feel almost lifelike, blurring the line between the dream world and reality. Vivid dreams can be exhilarating and disconcerting, often reflecting our deepest emotions and experiences. For instance, you might dream of a significant life event, like a childhood memory or a major personal achievement, with every detail rendered startlingly. These dreams can be so impactful that they influence your mood and thoughts the following day.

Often occurring during intense emotional or psychological stress, vivid dreams can serve as a release valve for the subconscious, allowing us to process and navigate our feelings in a safe, abstract space. They can also be a source of creativity and inspiration, as their vivid nature can spark new ideas and perspectives. Vivid dreams are a testament to the power and complexity of our dreaming minds, offering a rich and colourful experience of the subconscious.

In our quest to understand the myriad types of dreams we encounter, we gain invaluable insights into the enigmatic voyages we undertake each night. Every dream, be it a lucid escapade where we're acutely aware of our dream state, a terrifying nightmare that jolts us awake, or a cryptic narrative woven with complex symbols, serves as a distinct portal into our subconscious mind. These dreams are more than mere figments of our imagination; they are reflective narratives that hold the essence of our innermost thoughts, fears, and longings. As we navigate through the landscapes of lucid dreams, face the daunting shadows in our nightmares, decipher the intricate symbols of our subconscious, or bask in the vividness of a particularly memorable dream, we embark on a journey of self-discovery. Each dream is akin to a story, a unique chapter in our subconscious's vast, intricate tapestry, each strand intertwined with the fibres of our emotions, experiences, and the essence of our being. Through the lens of our dreams, we can glimpse into the uncharted territories of our psyche, uncover hidden aspects of ourselves, and embark on a path of introspection and understanding.

Let us carry forward the understanding that every dream,

in its unique way, is a guide, teacher, and mirror, reflecting the multifaceted nature of our lives and leading us towards a deeper comprehension of who we are and our journey.

CHAPTER FIVE

Dreams in Hindu Philosophy

In the richly woven narrative of Hindu philosophy, dreams are esteemed as a bridge connecting the tangible realities of life with the enigmatic depths of consciousness. As you immerse yourself in this exploration, envision embarking on an enlightening voyage that transcends the ordinary, reaching into the mystical essence of existence. Dreams, within this ancient wisdom, are not just ephemeral night visions; they are profound channels through which the soul communicates, offering glimpses into the deeper layers of our being. The revered texts of Hinduism, such as the Bhagavad Gita and the Upanishads, often discuss dreams as instrumental in gaining self-knowledge and spiritual insight. In the Bhagavad Gita, Lord Krishna speaks of the power of understanding the self, a concept deeply connected to the revelations experienced in dreams. The Mandukya Upanishad explicitly discusses the state of dreaming (Swapna) as a stage of consciousness that provides insights into the true nature of reality and the self. These ancient scriptures guide us to view our dreams as sacred encounters, illuminating the path to self-discovery and enlightenment. As you delve deeper into the teachings of Hindu philosophy, let each dream you recall be a step closer to unravelling the mysteries of your inner world, guided by the timeless wisdom of these spiritual texts.

The Three States of Consciousness

In Hindu philosophy, the three states of consciousness offer a profound framework for understanding our existence. These states are Jagrat (waking state), Swapna (dream state), and Sushupti (deep sleep state). Envision your daily cycle: you wake up in Jagrat, engaging with the world, making decisions, and experiencing life through your senses and intellect. Here, your consciousness is outwardly focused, dealing with the tangible aspects of your existence. As night falls and you drift asleep, you enter Swapna, the dream state. This is where the vivid world of dreams unfolds, a realm where the usual rules of physics and logic don't apply. For example, you might dream of talking to a loved one who has passed away, experiencing a conversation that feels incredibly real, though it defies the waking world's reality. This state provides a unique window into your subconscious, revealing fears, desires, and hidden aspects of your psyche. Then, in the deepest part of your sleep cycle, you enter Sushupti, the dreamless deep sleep state. In this state, there is no dreaming, sense of self, or cognition. It's a profound rest state that rejuvenates the mind and body. The Upanishads speak of this state as closest to the true, unmanifested essence of the self, a glimpse into our existence's boundless and formless aspect. According to Hindu philosophy, these three states of consciousness offer insights into the nature of reality and our self, each revealing different aspects of our being and the universe we inhabit.

Dreams in the Upanishads

In the Upanishads, ancient and revered texts of Hindu philosophy, dreams are explored with profound depth and insight, providing a unique perspective on their significance. These texts often discuss dreams as a realm where the soul is free from the constraints of the physical world, allowing for an exploration of deeper truths. For instance, the Brihadaranyaka Upanishad delves into the nature of dreams, suggesting that the soul detaches itself from the physical body and experiences its reality in the dream state. This is a realm where the conventional rules of time and space do not apply, enabling the dreamer to travel to distant lands or converse with departed ancestors. These experiences, though occurring in a dream, hold profound meaning, offering insights into the self and the universe. The Upanishads also touch upon the concept of 'Maya' or illusion, suggesting that just as dreams are real while they last, the waking world is a kind of dream, an illusionary play of the ultimate reality, Brahman. In a practical sense, this philosophy encourages introspection and mindfulness, urging us to look beyond the apparent and explore the deeper meanings of our dreams. By doing so, we can better understand our inner selves and the cosmic dance of creation and existence, as depicted in these ancient texts.

Dreams and the Godly Connection

In Hindu philosophy, dreams are often viewed as a sacred intersection where the divine realm touches the human consciousness. This connection is vividly illustrated in numerous Hindu scriptures, where dreams act as channels for divine communication. A quintessential example can be found in the epic Mahabharata, where King Dhritarashtra is visited by ominous dreams foretelling the doom of his lineage, interpreted as divine omens. These narratives are not mere folklore but resonate deeply in Hindu culture. It's common in Hindu households to hear tales of individuals receiving guidance or warnings from deities in their dreams. Such an experience might involve dreaming of a deity offering advice or comfort during a time of distress, prompting the dreamer upon waking to undertake a pilgrimage or perform specific rituals, interpreting the dream as a divine message. This seamless blending of the divine into the dream world is central to Hindu thought, suggesting dreams are a significant spiritual medium. They're not just a psychological phenomenon but a realm where gods and mortals converse, divine wisdom is imparted, and the spiritual journey is nurtured. These godly connections in dreams underscore the profound spiritual dimension of dreaming in Hindu culture, where dreams are revered as a window to divine wisdom and guidance.

Karma and Dreams

In Hindu philosophy, the intricate concept of Karma is deeply intertwined with the realm of dreams, offering a unique lens through which the subconscious mind communicates. Karma, the law of cause and effect, holds that every action has consequences, shaping our present and future experiences. Dreams are often seen as reflections or manifestations of this karmic cycle. For instance, imagine repeatedly dreaming about a situation where you're helping or harming someone. Such dreams could be interpreted as echoes of past karmic actions, signalling unresolved issues or lessons your soul is trying to process. These dreams might reveal hidden aspects of your character or past actions, urging introspection and self-correction to balance past karmic debts. In this context, dreams serve as a mirror, reflecting our actions' moral and ethical implications and their repercussions on our life's journey. This connection between karma and dreams reminds us that our subconscious mind holds not just our immediate thoughts and fears but also deeper, more spiritual concerns related to our life's path and the cosmic law of karma. It encourages a view of dreams as not just random neural activities but as meaningful insights into our spiritual evolution and moral compass.

The Path to Self-Realization

In the rich fabric of Hindu philosophy, dreams are often considered vital signposts on the path to self-realization, a journey towards understanding and uniting with one's true self. This quest for self-realization, central to Hindu thought, sees dreams as a reflective surface for the inner workings of the soul. For example, envision a dream where you're climbing a steep mountain. The climb is arduous, but the summit promises a breathtaking view. In the context of self-realization, this dream could symbolize your journey towards higher consciousness – the mountain being the challenges and struggles, and the summit representing enlightenment or self-awareness. Hindu texts, such as the Vedas and Upanishads, often discuss the importance of introspection and understanding the self, and dreams are seen as a medium through which deeper insights about one's nature and purpose can be gleaned. They encourage exploring the symbolism and emotions of your dreams, as these can provide clues to your deepest desires, fears, and life's purpose. Dreams, in this philosophy, are not mere byproducts of sleep but are considered meaningful experiences that can guide you towards realizing your true potential and understanding the fundamental nature of your existence. This perspective transforms the way one views dreams from mere subconscious activities to profound experiences that contribute to one's spiritual and personal growth.

Now, we have a deeper understanding of how dreams are perceived in this rich and ancient tradition. They are not mere figments of our imagination but are seen as profound channels for spiritual insight, self-discovery, and divine communication. In the Hindu worldview, dreams offer a unique perspective on our lives, reflecting our deepest desires, fears, and karmic imprints. They guide the path to self-realization, helping us unravel the mysteries of our subconscious and understand the intricate dance of the cosmos.

This exploration of dreams in Hindu philosophy illuminates how cultural contexts can deeply influence our understanding of the dream world. As we transition to the next chapter, we will expand our horizons further, exploring how different cultures worldwide interpret the enigmatic realm of dreams. Each culture's unique beliefs, traditions, and philosophies contribute to a diverse tapestry of interpretations and understandings.

From the shamanic dream practices of indigenous cultures to the psychoanalytic theories of the West, we will delve into many perspectives. We'll see how various societies have sought to understand and interpret dreams and used them for healing, guidance, and even as portals to other dimensions. The shift from Hindu philosophy's spiritual and introspective approach to a broader global view will offer a fascinating contrast and complement our understanding of dreams. We will discover that while the interpretation of dreams may vary widely across different cultures, the quest to understand them is a common thread that connects humanity across time and space.

CHAPTER SIX

Global Perspectives on Dreams

As we transition from the mystical insights of Hindu philosophy, our journey into the realm of dreams takes a broader sweep, encompassing the rich tapestry of global perspectives. This exploration is an invitation to traverse the globe, from the ancient wisdom of long-gone civilizations to the intricate beliefs of contemporary cultures. Each society and era brings its unique understanding of the phenomenon of dreams, weaving them intricately into its cultural fabric. In ancient civilizations, dreams were often seen as divine messages or omens, integral to spiritual and daily life. Fast forward to modern times, where dreams remain significant, though often viewed through a more psychological or symbolic lens. This chapter is more than a mere compilation of various interpretations; it's a journey into the heart of our shared human experience. It highlights the universal nature of dreams, showcasing how dreams remain a common yet profoundly personal experience despite our diverse backgrounds and beliefs. They are a testament to our shared humanity, revealing that, across cultures and ages, dreams continue to inspire, guide, and mystify us in equal measure.

Indigenous Wisdom: Dreams as Spiritual Guidance
In the rich panorama of indigenous cultures, dreams are revered not just as nightly experiences but as vital conduits for spiritual guidance and wisdom. For these communities, dreams are a sacred dialogue with the spiritual world, offering insights, guidance, and healing. Take, for instance, the Native American tradition, where a dream about a specific animal, such as a wolf or an eagle, is not merely a dream but a visitation from a spirit guide or totem. Such a dream might be interpreted as a guidance message, calling for qualities the animal represents — like the wolf's intuition or the eagle's perspective. In Australian Aboriginal culture, the concept of 'Dreamtime' is fundamental. It's a profound spiritual belief system where dreams are a window to another world of ancestors and creation stories, shaping their understanding of the world and their place in it. These cultures often hold dream-sharing as a communal practice, where insights from dreams are discussed with elders or shamans, who help interpret their meanings and implications. In these traditions, dreams are not just personal experiences but woven into the community's spiritual fabric, offering guidance, foresight, and a deeper connection to the ancestors and the natural world. For indigenous people, dreams are a sacred pathway, a bridge between the physical and spiritual realms, deeply embedded in their cultural and spiritual life.

Ancient Egypt: The Gateway to Divination
In Ancient Egypt, one of the cradles of civilization, dreams were revered as mystical gateways to divination and

prophetic insight. The Egyptians believed dreams were messages from the gods, laden with symbolic significance and often foretelling the future. Picture an ancient Egyptian priest sleeping in a temple dedicated to a god-like Thoth or Anubis, seeking divine revelations through dreams. For instance, dreaming of the Nile River overflowing might have been interpreted as a sign of abundant harvest or a warning of impending flood and hardship. The Egyptians meticulously recorded and interpreted these dreams, often employing complex symbolism intertwined with their rich mythology. Dreams of Pharaohs and commoners alike were considered significant; they were thought to hold the keys to vital decisions and state affairs. The 'dream incubation' practice was common, where individuals would sleep in sacred spaces, hoping to receive divine messages through their dreams. This ancient culture's view of dreams highlights their deep integration into the fabric of religious and daily life, treating them as a crucial link between the mortal world and the divine realm and an essential tool for guidance and insight.

Greek and Roman Views: Dreams as Omens

In the classical world of ancient Greece and Rome, dreams were held in high esteem as omens, carrying messages from the gods. These civilizations believed that dreams could foretell the future and provide divine counsel. For instance, in Greek culture, a dream of a crashing thunderbolt might be interpreted as a warning from Zeus, the king of gods, indicating impending judgment or the need for moral rectification. Similarly, the Romans viewed dreams as significant omens affecting personal life and the empire's fate. A Roman general might dream of an eagle - a symbol of Jupiter and representing victory and strength - which could be interpreted as a favourable omen for an upcoming battle. Dreams were so integral to these cultures that they established sacred spaces, like the Temple of Asclepius in Greece, where people would sleep and receive healing dreams sent by the gods, a practice known as 'incubation.' Renowned historical figures, such as Alexander the Great, were known to have been influenced by prophetic dreams, guiding their decisions and shaping their destinies. This belief in dreams as omens reflects a broader understanding in these cultures of a universe where gods intimately interacted with human affairs, and dreams were a key medium for this divine-human communication.

Islamic Insights: Dreams as a Blend of the Spiritual and the Mundane

In the tapestry of Islamic culture, dreams hold a special place, blending the spiritual with the mundane and offering deeply revered insights. Islamic tradition categorizes dreams into three types: true dreams (ru'ya), which are divine messages; false dreams, which stem from anxiety or the subconscious; and dreams from the devil, which are misleading or disturbing. For example, a Muslim might dream of standing in a lush, verdant garden, symbolizing the soul's journey towards Jannah (paradise), and take it as encouragement to lead a righteous life. The significance of dreams in Islam is underscored by the Prophet Muhammad's own experiences, as some revelations in the Quran were conveyed through dreams. Dreams in Islamic culture are a means of divine communication and a source of guidance and reassurance. They are often shared with scholars or interpreters for analysis, reflecting their importance in daily life and decision-making. For instance, a dream of flying could be interpreted as a sign of spiritual elevation, while seeing water might symbolize knowledge and wisdom. This reverence for dreams in Islam reflects a broader understanding of the human experience, where the spiritual and the mundane are intricately linked, and dreams are a valuable window into this interwoven reality.

The Western Psychoanalytic Approach

Dreams take on a different but equally fascinating significance in the Western world, particularly through the lens of psychoanalytic theory. Pioneered by figures like Sigmund Freud and Carl Jung, this approach views dreams as crucial windows into the unconscious mind. Freud famously theorized that dreams are expressions of repressed desires and unfulfilled wishes. Imagine dreaming about missing a train; Freud might interpret this as a symbol of missed opportunities or a hidden desire to escape some aspect of your life. On the other hand, Carl Jung perceived dreams as more than personal desires, viewing them as a bridge to the collective unconscious, a repository of universal human experiences and archetypes. For instance, if you dream of a snake, Jung might see it not just as a personal fear or desire but as a symbol of transformation and renewal, a motif common across various cultures and mythologies. This psychoanalytic perspective delves into the symbolic language of dreams, decoding them to uncover deeper emotional and psychological truths. In this view, dreams are not mere byproducts of sleep but meaningful narratives that reflect our deepest fears, conflicts, and aspirations. They offer a pathway to self-awareness and personal development, providing a unique glimpse into the complexities of the human psyche.

As we traverse these global perspectives, it becomes clear that despite the diversity in interpretations, dreams are universally regarded as significant. They are bridges between the physical and the spiritual, the individual and the collective, the earthly and the divine. Each culture brings its unique lens, yet all converge on the idea that dreams are vital to the human experience. In the next chapter, we'll delve deeper into how these varied interpretations can be integrated into our understanding of dreams, providing a richer, more comprehensive view of this fascinating aspect of our lives.

CHAPTER SEVEN

Symbolism in Dreams

Let us venture into the captivating world of your dreams, where every image, character, and scenario transcends mere visual impressions, unfolding rich layers of meaning and symbolism. This journey into the heart of your dream world is akin to learning a new language — the language of symbolism, where each element is a word, each scene a sentence, revealing the deeper narratives of your subconscious mind. In dreams, a simple object like a key or a door can hold profound significance, a character you meet might represent an aspect of yourself or someone in your life, and the scenarios you find yourself in often mirror your innermost thoughts and emotions. Let's embark on this insightful exploration together, unravelling the symbolic messages hidden in the tapestry of your dreams. Whether it's a recurring dream that leaves you pondering its meaning or a fleeting image that lingers in your waking thoughts, each has the potential to offer personal revelations and insights. By decoding these symbols, we can uncover the underlying fears and desires that drive us and the hopes and aspirations that propel us forward. This journey is not just about interpretation; it's about connecting with the deeper parts of yourself, understanding the unspoken words of your subconscious, and gaining a clearer perspective on your life's path.

Water: The Flow of Emotions

Water in dreams often symbolizes your emotional state. Imagine standing by a calm, serene lake in your dream. This might reflect a sense of peace or emotional clarity in your life. Conversely, dreaming of turbulent, stormy seas could indicate feelings of emotional upheaval or stress. The state of the water in your dream mirrors your inner emotional world, providing clues to how you're navigating your emotional journey.

Flying: A Desire for Freedom

Have you ever dreamt of soaring through the sky, unbounded and free? Flying in dreams is often interpreted as a desire for freedom, whether from a situation, a relationship, or internal constraints. It can also symbolize ambition and your aspirations to rise above your current circumstances. The exhilaration or fear you experience while flying in the dream can provide further insight into your feelings towards freedom and autonomy in your waking life.

Falling: Loss of Control

Falling dreams are common and can be quite jarring. They usually symbolize a loss of control in some aspect of your life. You might feel insecure or unstable in a job, relationship, or personal matter. The sensation of falling can also represent a fear of failure or an anxiety about not meeting others' expectations.

Being Chased: Avoiding an Issue

Dreams of being chased often point to an issue you're

avoiding in your waking life. The pursuer in the dream could represent a problem, a person, or an emotion you don't want to face. Whether you confront the pursuer or continue to run, your reaction to the dream can offer insight into how you deal with challenges or conflicts.

Houses: The Self and Identity

A house in a dream often represents the dreamer. Different rooms might symbolize different aspects of your personality or life. For example, an attic could represent hidden memories, while a basement might symbolize neglected or subconscious aspects of yourself. The condition of the house in your dream – whether it's well-kept, in disrepair, or unfamiliar – can offer clues about your self-esteem and personal growth.

Roads and Pathways: Life's Journey

Dreaming about roads or pathways often symbolizes your journey through life. A smooth, straight road might suggest that you're confident and clear about your life direction. In contrast, a winding or obstructed path could indicate uncertainty or challenges you are facing. The roads in your dreams can mirror your feelings about your life's path – are you lost, moving forward confidently, or facing a crossroad?

Animals: Instinctual Aspects of Self

Animals in dreams can represent different aspects of your personality, often relating to your instinctual nature. For instance, dreaming of a lion might symbolize courage and strength, while a snake could represent transformation or hidden fears. The animal's behaviour in your dream is also significant – is it friendly, aggressive, or elusive? These interactions can provide insights into how you're dealing with your primal instincts and emotions.

Clothing: Self-Image and Identity

The clothes you wear in a dream often reflect your self-image and how you want others to see you. Dreaming about wearing formal attire might suggest you're preparing for an important event or want to make a good impression. Alternatively, being inappropriately dressed for a situation could indicate inadequacy or unpreparedness. Clothes in dreams can also symbolize your roles and how comfortable you are in those roles.

Teeth: Power and Confidence

Dreams involving teeth – such as losing or having dental issues – are surprisingly common. These dreams can symbolize concerns about appearance and social acceptance, powerlessness, or anxiety about a significant life change. Teeth are tools for biting, chewing, and speaking, so issues with teeth in dreams can point to feelings of impotence or inability to process a situation.

Death: Endings and New Beginnings

While dreaming about death can be unsettling, it often symbolizes the end of something and the start of something new. This could be the end of a relationship, a job, or a phase in life and the beginning of a new journey. Death in dreams can also represent transformation and personal growth.

Flying Objects: Ambitions and Desires

Dreams featuring flying objects, whether aeroplanes, balloons, or even flying carpets, often symbolize your ambitions and desires. Soaring high in the sky can represent your aspirations and the freedom to chase your dreams. Conversely, a crashing or malfunctioning flying object might reflect fears of failure or losing control in your pursuit of these ambitions.

Fire: Passion or Destruction

Fire in dreams can have dual interpretations. On one hand, it may represent passion, energy, and transformation. Dreaming of a controlled fire, like a cosy campfire or a lit candle, might symbolize warmth, inspiration, and enlightenment. On the other hand, an uncontrolled fire, like a wildfire, might represent anger, destruction, or unchecked emotions running rampant in your life.

Children: Innocence and Potential

Dreaming of children can symbolize innocence, pure potential, and new beginnings. The children in your dreams might represent your inner child, pointing to aspects of yourself that are unspoiled and hopeful. Alternatively, they could symbolize a project or aspect of your life still in its developmental stages, requiring care and attention.

Clocks and Time: Life's Progression

Clocks and the concept of time in dreams often reflect your concerns about life's progression. A fast-moving clock might symbolize the feeling that time is running out or life is passing by too quickly. On the other hand, a stopped or broken clock could indicate a sense of stagnation or a pause in personal growth or progress.

Bridges: Transition and Connection

Bridges in dreams often symbolize transition and

connection. Crossing a bridge can represent a significant life change or a transitional phase. It might also symbolize the connection between two states of being or aspects of your personality. The condition and stability of the bridge in your dream can offer additional insights into your feelings about these transitions or connections.

The symbolism in dreams provides a rich and multifaceted language through which your subconscious communicates. Understanding these symbols can offer profound insights into your emotional and psychological state, guiding you to greater self-awareness. As you continue on your journey of dream exploration, remember that the most profound meanings will always be shaped by your personal experiences, emotions, and context. Your dreams are a unique and personal life narrative, reflecting your deepest fears, desires, and everything. Embrace this journey with an open mind, and let your dreams guide you towards deeper self-understanding and personal growth.

CHAPTER EIGHT

Cultural Variations in Symbolism

Embarking on exploring dream symbolism, we must acknowledge the rich tapestry of interpretations that vary widely across cultures. This journey is not merely about deciphering differing meanings; it's an immersive experience into the diverse and vibrant spectrum of human thought and tradition. As we traverse various cultural landscapes, we discover that a single symbol in a dream can unravel into many meanings, each deeply rooted in its cultural context. For instance, the snake image may evoke fear and betrayal in one culture while it symbolizes wisdom and healing in another. The moon, often a symbol of mystery and the feminine, might represent divine connection in one society but could symbolize change or impermanence in another. Understanding these cultural variations in dream symbolism is a journey into empathy and global awareness, broadening our perspectives and deepening our appreciation for how different people around the world connect with the universal experience of dreaming. Each interpretation offers a unique lens, coloured by historical, spiritual, and social influences, allowing us to see beyond our own experiences and embrace a more inclusive understanding of the world of dream interpretation. Let's explore how the same symbol can carry different connotations in various cultural contexts, enriching your understanding of the vast world of dream interpretation.

The Serpent: Transformation or Temptation

Consider the symbol of the serpent. In Western cultures, influenced by Judeo-Christian narratives, the snake often symbolizes temptation or evil, as seen in the story of Adam and Eve. However, in Hindu culture, the serpent, or 'Naga,' is revered, symbolizing fertility, rebirth, and even immortality. Imagine dreaming of a serpent. You might interpret it in the West as a warning of betrayal or deceit. In contrast, it could be seen as a sign of spiritual awakening or transformation in Eastern cultures.

Water: Life Source or Chaos

Water is another symbol with varying cultural interpretations. In many Eastern cultures, water is often seen as a symbol of life, purity, and renewal. For instance, in Japanese culture, water is associated with purity and is an integral part of Shinto purification rituals. Conversely, in some Western interpretations, particularly influenced by Biblical narratives like Noah's flood, water can symbolize chaos, destruction, or overwhelming emotions. Dreaming of calm, clear water might be comforting in one culture, while stormy seas might be considered a warning sign in another.

Birds: Messengers or Omens

Birds are often seen as symbols of freedom and transcendence. In Native American cultures, specific birds like the eagle or the raven are considered sacred and are seen as messengers from the spiritual world. In contrast, in some European traditions, birds, especially blackbirds like crows or ravens, can be seen as omens of bad news or death. So, a dream of a bird can be a message of spiritual guidance in one culture but a warning in another.

The Color White: Purity or Mourning

Even colours in dreams can have different cultural meanings. In many Western cultures, white is associated with purity, peace, and weddings. However, in some Eastern cultures, like in China and India, white is the colour of mourning and funerals. Dreaming of a white object or wearing white can have divergent interpretations based on these cultural contexts.

The Sun: Life-Giver or Harbinger of Trouble

In many cultures, the sun is a powerful symbol in dreams, often representing life, vitality, and energy. For instance, in ancient Egyptian culture, the sun was personified by the god Ra, representing creation, growth, and renewal. However, in some desert cultures, where the sun can be a relentless force, it might symbolize harshness, trouble, or overwhelming situations. Dreaming of the sun in these contrasting cultures can elicit feelings of hope and inspiration or anxiety and challenge.

Trees: Connection or Isolation

Trees in dreams often symbolize growth, stability, and connection to one's roots. In Celtic cultures, trees are sacred and are seen as bridges between the heavens and the earth. Dreaming of a flourishing tree might be interpreted as a sign of personal growth or ancestral strength. However, in some urban-centric cultures, a solitary tree might symbolize isolation or feeling out of place, particularly if it appears in a stark or barren landscape.

The Crossroads: Decision or Danger

Dreaming of standing at a crossroads is a potent symbol that can vary in interpretation. In many Western cultures, a crossroads can symbolize a significant life decision or a pivotal point in one's life journey. However, in various African and Caribbean cultures, crossroads are often associated with the spiritual realm and can signify where the material world meets the spiritual, sometimes indicating danger or the need for caution.

Mountains: Challenge or Enlightenment

Mountains in dreams are often seen as symbols of challenges, obstacles, or high aspirations. In Western cultures, climbing a mountain in a dream might symbolize overcoming challenges or achieving a high goal. In contrast, in some Eastern cultures, mountains are sacred and are often associated with spiritual enlightenment and withdrawal from the material world. Thus, a dream involving mountains can be interpreted as a journey towards spiritual awakening or a call to face and overcome personal challenges.

Food: Nourishment or Excess

Food in dreams can represent nourishment, abundance, and family connections. In cultures where food is central to family and community life, dreaming of a feast might symbolize togetherness and celebration. However, in societies where there is a focus on dieting and body image, dreaming about food might represent guilt, indulgence, or self-image issues.

Animals as Totems and Symbols

In many indigenous cultures, animals in dreams are not just random figures; they are totems, representing spiritual guides, clan identity, or personal traits. For instance, a Native American might dream of a bear, symbolising strength, leadership, and healing. In contrast, in some Eastern cultures, dreaming of a tiger might be seen as a sign of imminent danger or powerful enemies, while in other contexts, it might symbolize strength and royal dignity.

Water Bodies: Rivers, Seas, and Lakes

The interpretation of water bodies in dreams varies greatly across cultures. In many Asian cultures, rivers symbolise life's journey, carrying ancestral spirits and life-giving energy. Dreaming of a river might be interpreted as a sign of life's flow and the continuity of generations. In contrast, in Western psychoanalytic thought, large bodies of water, like seas or oceans, might symbolize the unconscious mind, with its hidden depths and unknown contents.

Clothing and Attire

Clothing in dreams can have cultural-specific interpretations related to social status, profession, or identity. In a traditional society, dreaming of wearing ceremonial or traditional clothing might signify a connection to one's roots or an upcoming rite of passage. In modern, fashion-conscious societies, dreaming about wearing designer or fashionable clothing could represent social status, self-image, or aspirations.

Architectural Structures

Buildings and architectural structures in dreams can also carry varied cultural connotations. Dreaming of ancient temples or pyramids might connect one to historical roots, spiritual aspirations, or past life experiences in certain cultures. In modern Western contexts, skyscrapers or modern buildings might symbolize ambitions, modern life's complexities, or feelings of being overwhelmed by one's environment.

Weather Patterns

Weather in dreams often reflects emotional states or foretells changes, but these interpretations can vary widely. In some cultures, dreaming of rain might be seen as a positive sign of cleansing, renewal, and fertility. In others, it could symbolize sadness, depression, or a period of difficulty. Similarly, storms can symbolize personal turmoil or, conversely, the clearing of obstacles and renewal.

Flowers: Symbols of Growth and Decay

In dreams, flowers often symbolize growth, beauty, and the natural cycle of life. Dreaming of blooming flowers in Western cultures might represent love, happiness, or new beginnings. However, in some Asian cultures, certain flowers, like the lotus, hold profound spiritual meanings, often symbolizing enlightenment and purity of the heart and mind. Conversely, wilting or dying flowers in dreams could represent loss, fading beauty, or the passage of time, but this interpretation can vary significantly across different cultural contexts.

The Moon: Mystery and Change

The moon in dreams can be a powerful symbol with varied

cultural interpretations. In many Western cultures, the moon often symbolizes femininity, mystery, and the rhythms of time. Dreaming of a full moon might represent completeness, clarity, or emotional enlightenment. In contrast, in some Eastern cultures, the moon can symbolise impermanence, change, or even unattainable desire, as expressed in many poems and artworks.

Vehicles: Journey of Life

Vehicles in dreams, be it cars, boats, or trains, often represent life's journey. In Western societies, dreaming about driving a car might symbolize personal control and ambition. In contrast, in other cultures, the type of vehicle and its condition could have specific meanings. For instance, a boat might represent a spiritual journey in Eastern cultures, reflecting the passage through life or across the metaphysical realms.

Doors and Gateways

Dreaming of doors or gateways can symbolize opportunities, transitions, or choices. In some cultures, an open door might represent a welcome opportunity or a new path, while a closed door could symbolize missed opportunities or barriers. In many Middle Eastern cultures, doors are often seen as protective symbols, representing the threshold between the public and private spheres or between the known and the unknown.

Shadows and Darkness

Shadows and darkness in dreams are often associated with the unknown, hidden fears, or aspects of the self that are not fully acknowledged. However, cultural interpretations can vary greatly. In some Western interpretations, shadows might represent the 'darker' aspects of the psyche, as per Jungian psychology. In various Eastern cultures, shadows can be seen as representations of transience, impermanence, or the yin aspect of yin and yang, symbolizing passivity, femininity, and receptivity.

Mountains and Valleys

The symbolism of mountains and valleys in dreams can vary greatly across cultures. In many Western cultures, mountains are often seen as obstacles to overcome or goals to be achieved, reflecting a focus on individual achievement and conquest. In contrast, Eastern philosophies might view mountains as sacred spaces, symbols of spiritual attainment and tranquillity. Conversely, valleys might represent protection and comfort in some cultures, while they could symbolize being stuck or lost in others.

The Forest: Mystery and the Subconscious

Forests in dreams often represent the unknown or the subconscious mind. In Western fairy tales and folklore, forests are places of danger and mystery. Dreaming of a forest might symbolize entering the unknown territories of your mind. In contrast, the forest symbolises life, interconnectedness, and the ancestors' wisdom in many indigenous cultures. Dreaming of being in a forest might be interpreted as a journey of self-discovery guided by ancestral knowledge.

The Color Red: Passion or Warning

The colour red in dreams can have many meanings across different cultures. In Western societies, red is often associated with passion, danger, or anger. Dreaming of red might symbolize intense emotions or a warning sign.

However, in many Asian cultures, red is a colour of good luck, happiness, and celebration. A dream featuring red could then be interpreted as an auspicious sign or a symbol of prosperity.

Bridges and Crossing Over

Bridges in dreams often symbolize transition or crossing over into a new phase of life. In many Western narratives, bridges can represent a critical life decision or a pivotal point of change. However, in various Eastern philosophies, bridges may symbolize the path to enlightenment or the connection between the physical and spiritual realms. Crossing a bridge in a dream can thus hold different implications based on cultural perspectives.

Animals as Cultural Icons

The cultural significance of specific animals in dreams can greatly influence their interpretation. For example, an eagle in a dream might symbolize freedom and strength in many Western cultures. However, in some Native American tribes, the eagle is a sacred symbol, representing a spiritual connection to the divine. Similarly, the elephant in a dream can be seen as a symbol of wisdom and reliability in Western contexts, while in Hindu culture, it is associated with the god Ganesha and symbolizes good luck and the removal of obstacles.

Exploring cultural variations in dream symbolism enriches our understanding of the human psyche. It reveals how deeply our cultural backgrounds and experiences influence our interpretation of the symbolic language of dreams. Recognizing and appreciating these cultural differences allows us to view our dreams through a more nuanced and comprehensive lens. It opens us up to a world where the same symbol can have manifold meanings, each offering unique insights into our subconscious minds and the collective human experience. As we embrace this diversity in dream interpretation, we gain a deeper, more empathetic understanding of our dreams and those of others from different cultural backgrounds.

CHAPTER NINE

Dreams and Emotions

Venturing into the captivating world of "Dreams and Emotions" is akin to stepping through a portal into a realm where your most profound emotions are not just felt but vividly enacted. In this realm, each night becomes a stage where the drama of your subconscious unfolds, painting your innermost fears, longings, and joys with the vibrant brushstrokes of dream imagery. Imagine your feelings as characters in this play, each one expressing aspects of your psyche in symbolic form. A dream where you're lost in a vast forest, for instance, might symbolize feelings of uncertainty or exploration in your life. A joyful flight across the sky could reflect a newfound sense of freedom or aspiration. In this exploration, we will unravel how your emotional state intricately weaves the fabric of your dreams, and conversely, how these dreams can cast a significant impact on your waking emotional life. It's a bidirectional dance where dreams can be both a reflection of your current emotional state and a catalyst for profound emotional change. Whether processing hidden anxieties, celebrating unacknowledged victories, or providing an outlet for unexpressed sorrow, your dreams are a powerful tool for emotional insight and transformation, offering a deeper understanding of your emotional health and well-being.

The Reflection of Daily Emotions

Picture yourself concluding a day overwhelmed with stress and anxiety, carrying the weight of the day's troubles to bed. As you drift into sleep, the turmoil of your waking hours begins to seep into the tapestry of your dreams. You might find yourself in a relentless chase, desperately trying to escape an unseen pursuer, or wandering aimlessly in an unfamiliar place, feeling lost and alone. These dreams act as a vivid mirror, reflecting and often magnifying the emotions that dominate your waking life. The intensity and imagery of the dream — the speed of the chase, the labyrinthine complexity of the paths you tread — all symbolize the depth and nature of your stress and anxiety. It's as if your subconscious mind is dramatizing your emotional state, offering you a stark, symbolic representation of your waking challenges. In doing so, these dreams provide a unique space for emotional processing. They allow you to confront and engage with your feelings in a setting removed from the constraints of reality. This can often lead to a better understanding of these emotions, shining a light on underlying issues and sometimes offering a sense of catharsis or resolution that might be harder to achieve in the hustle of daily life.

Nightmares and Unresolved Feelings

Nightmares serve as powerful windows into the deeper, often unresolved emotions that simmer beneath the surface of our conscious minds. Envision yourself in a dream where you're caught in an unending fall, a sensation of both weightlessness and dread gripping you as you plummet through an endless void. This harrowing experience in the dream world could be a stark symbol of feelings of helplessness or a pervasive fear of failure that haunts your waking life. Such nightmares are like emotional alarms, bringing to light the most profound fears and anxieties that you may not fully acknowledge or understand when you're awake. They provide a visceral, emotional experience that can be far more impactful than mere thoughts or reflections. By presenting these fears in such a vivid, often unsettling manner, nightmares compel you to confront these hidden emotions head-on. They create a space for you to engage with and process these feelings, sometimes revealing deeper insecurities or unresolved conflicts that are influencing your emotional well-being. This confrontation, while often uncomfortable, can be a crucial step in understanding and resolving the underlying issues, offering a path to emotional clarity and healing.

Joyful Dreams and Aspirations
At the opposite end of the emotional spectrum, dreams can be a wellspring of joy and a reflection of our most cherished aspirations. Imagine a dream where you experience a heartwarming reunion with a long-lost friend or a loved one, or where you triumphantly achieve a long-sought-after goal. These scenarios, unfolding within the dream realm, often mirror your innermost yearnings and sources of happiness. The emotions experienced in these dreams - the elation of a heartfelt embrace or the surge of pride in an accomplishment - can be so intense and vivid that their warmth and positivity linger with you throughout your waking day. They imbue you with a sense of hope and motivation, serving as reminders of the joy and fulfillment that life holds. Such dreams can be particularly impactful during challenging times, providing a much-needed respite

and a rejuvenating boost to your morale. They underscore the incredible power of positive emotions in our dreams, illustrating how our subconscious can be a source of not just reflection and resolution but also of celebration and inspiration, highlighting the full spectrum of human emotion that our dream world encapsulates.

Emotional Release in Dreams

Dreams often function as a vital emotional outlet, offering a sanctuary where the feelings and emotions we hold back in our daily lives can freely surface and express themselves. Picture a scenario where, in your dream, you find yourself overcome with tears, sobbing with an intensity that you seldom allow yourself in the waking world. Or perhaps, you experience a dream filled with laughter, where you chuckle and guffaw with a freedom and abandon that's rarely found in your daytime hours. These emotional expressions within dreams are not just random occurrences; they are crucial for maintaining your emotional well-being. They act as a release valve, allowing you to vent pent-up emotions and feelings in a safe and unconstrained environment. This release is often therapeutic, helping you to manage and balance your emotional state. It's as if your subconscious is providing you with a much-needed emotional outlet, a way to process and alleviate the stresses, anxieties, and repressions that accumulate in your conscious life. By experiencing these intense emotional expressions in your dreams, you're given an opportunity to confront and engage with your feelings, potentially leading to greater emotional clarity and health in your waking life.

Dreams as a Path to Healing

In the delicate aftermath of trauma or significant life

changes, dreams can emerge as a gentle yet powerful pathway to emotional healing. Imagine, in the quiet of the night, you find yourself in a dream, reuniting with a loved one who has passed away. In this ethereal meeting, you're afforded the opportunity to express the words left unsaid, to share moments of love and farewell that were never possible in waking reality. Similarly, dreams can take you back to past events, perhaps those you wish had unfolded differently. In the safe confines of the dream world, you get the chance to revisit these moments, not to change the past, but to understand, accept, and find peace with it. This process of dreaming can be deeply cathartic, providing a space where emotions related to grief, loss, or change can be acknowledged and processed. It's as if your subconscious is gently guiding you through the stages of healing, acknowledging your pain and loss, but also helping you to mend and move forward. These healing dreams offer a unique form of closure, one that's crafted by the mind's innate ability to seek resolution and peace, aiding in your journey towards emotional recovery and resilience.

Symbolic Expression of Emotions

Dreams have a unique language of their own, often communicating through symbols to convey the complexities of our emotions. Imagine you're in a dream where you find yourself caught in the midst of a brewing storm. This storm isn't just a weather phenomenon in your dream; it's a symbol, a metaphor for the emotional upheavals you might be experiencing in your waking life. The nature and intensity of the storm directly reflect the nature and intensity of your emotions. A gentle rain shower might represent transient worries or concerns, perhaps something that's bothering you but isn't overwhelmingly significant. In contrast, a violent, chaotic tempest in your dream could symbolize more profound, turbulent emotions — perhaps deep-seated anger, unresolved conflicts, or intense anxiety that you haven't yet come to terms with. The way you react to the storm in your dream, whether you seek shelter or stand fearlessly, can also provide clues about how you handle emotional distress in your waking life. Deciphering these symbolic representations in dreams can offer profound insights into your emotional well-being, helping you to understand and address your feelings with greater clarity and depth.

Emotional Processing During REM Sleep
In the depths of the Rapid Eye Movement (REM) phase of sleep, where the tapestry of dreams is most vividly woven, our brains engage in a dynamic process of emotional sorting and understanding. This stage of sleep becomes especially active and intense after days marked by strong emotional experiences. Picture a day that ends with a heated argument or an unexpectedly joyful encounter. As you drift into the REM phase, these emotionally laden events don't just fade away; instead, they often re-emerge in your dreams, sometimes replayed as they happened, other times reimagined or morphed into different scenarios. This nocturnal processing is much more than a mere replay of daily events; it's a crucial aspect of how your brain, and thereby your emotional self, processes and internalizes your experiences. The way these events are depicted in your dreams can offer insights into how you're really feeling about them, perhaps revealing underlying emotions or perspectives that weren't apparent in the heat of the moment. By engaging in this subconscious emotional processing, your mind works through the complexities of

your experiences, helping you to integrate and understand them as part of your ongoing emotional journey.

Dreams and Emotional Regulation

Dreams serve as a critical tool for the regulation and management of our emotions, acting as a safe and controlled space where we can freely experience and express feelings that might be repressed or unacknowledged in our waking life. Consider the experience of someone who typically struggles to show vulnerability or sadness in their daily interactions. In the dream world, this individual might find themselves in scenarios where they are openly weeping, releasing pent-up sorrow or frustration. This manifestation of crying in a dream isn't arbitrary; it's a subconscious mechanism that allows for the safe exploration and expression of these suppressed emotions. Within the boundaries of the dream, there's no need for the usual guards or facades we maintain in social settings. This emotional outpouring, though occurring in a dream, can have a therapeutic effect. It offers a way for the mind to process and work through emotions that need attention, albeit in a setting removed from the complexities and judgments of the real world. This aspect of dreaming is crucial for maintaining emotional balance, providing a unique and necessary outlet for emotional expression and processing.

Recurring Dreams and Emotional Patterns

Recurring dreams, particularly those imbued with intense emotions, often serve as indicators of persistent emotional themes or unresolved issues in our lives. Take, for example, the experience of repeatedly dreaming about being trapped or confined in some way. This isn't just a random motif;

it's likely a reflection of an ongoing sense of helplessness, entrapment, or frustration that you're encountering in your waking life. It could be related to a specific situation, such as a challenging relationship or a restrictive work environment, or it might symbolize broader feelings of being stuck or constrained. These recurring dreams are your subconscious mind's way of drawing attention to these issues, emphasizing their importance through their persistent recurrence. By closely observing and reflecting on these repetitive dream themes, you gain valuable insights into emotional patterns that might be playing out in your life. Understanding these patterns is a crucial step in addressing and resolving the underlying issues. It's like your dreams are sending you a message, a repeated signal, urging you to confront and work through the emotional challenges that are hindering your sense of freedom and well-being.

Dreams as a Reflection of Emotional Healing
In the transformative process of emotional healing, dreams often emerge as powerful allies, reflecting the strides you make and the resolutions you achieve. Consider the journey of overcoming a deep-seated fear or healing from a traumatic experience. Initially, this journey may be marked by nightmares or distressing dreams, mirroring the inner turmoil and struggle. However, as you navigate through the healing process, perhaps through therapy, self-reflection, or other forms of emotional work, a noticeable shift begins to occur in your dream landscape. The nightmares may gradually become less frequent and intense, or you might start experiencing dreams where you confront and conquer the very fears that once paralyzed you. Such changes in your dreaming patterns are far from trivial; they are

profound indicators of your emotional healing and growth. They signal that your subconscious mind is registering and adapting to the emotional work you're doing when you're awake. This evolving nature of your dreams serves as a barometer of your inner emotional state, offering encouragement and validation of your progress. It's as though your dreams are charting your journey, showing you how far you've come in overcoming obstacles and reclaiming your emotional well-being.

Premonitory Dreams and Anxiety

Sometimes, individuals encounter what might be termed as premonitory dreams, a phenomenon where the dream's emotional content — be it anxiety, fear, or another intense emotion — appears to echo or foreshadow real-life experiences. Imagine, for instance, dreaming vividly about misplacing a cherished possession, engulfed by a sense of loss and disarray. Subsequently, you might find yourself in a waking situation that triggers a remarkably similar emotional response, perhaps not involving a literal loss, but eliciting the same feeling of anxiety or disorientation. While these dreams are not prophetic in the traditional sense, they often mirror deep-seated worries or insecurities lurking in our subconscious. They may, in a way, be the mind's method of bracing for or processing potential real-life scenarios. This can be particularly true in periods of stress or transition, where our subconscious mind rehearses or simulates scenarios that we're apprehensive about, offering us a form of emotional rehearsal. This process underscores how intertwined our dreaming and waking emotional states are, with our dreams acting as a reflective and sometimes preparatory space for the challenges and experiences of our waking life.

Dreams as a Space for Safe Emotional Exploration
In the realm of dreams, we are granted access to a singular environment where the exploration of our emotions can occur with complete freedom and safety, unbound by the constraints and expectations of our waking reality. Imagine a scenario where, in your daily life, expressing certain emotions such as deep sadness, uncontrollable anger, or even exuberant joy might seem inappropriate or risky, potentially inviting judgment or misunderstanding from others. However, within the dreamscape, these same emotions can be expressed in their fullest intensity. Here, you can find yourself laughing with unbridled joy, weeping without restraint, expressing anger in its rawest form, or experiencing love with profound depth, all without the fear of repercussions or external judgment. This freedom to fully embody and express your emotions in dreams offers a powerful and often therapeutic release. It allows you to engage with and understand your emotions in a way that might not be possible in your waking life. This uninhibited emotional expression in dreams can be a crucial tool for self-discovery and emotional healing, providing insight into feelings you may not have fully acknowledged or understood. It's as if your dreams are a safe haven, a private stage where the complexities of your emotional life can be explored, experienced, and embraced in all their multifaceted glory.

Emotional Reconciliation in Dreams
At times, the world of dreams can transform into a healing space for emotional reconciliation, where unresolved conflicts and unspoken words find their expression. Picture a scenario where, in your waking life, you've had a falling

out or a deep-seated conflict with someone. This unresolved tension lingers in your subconscious, manifesting in your dreams. In these dreams, you might find yourself engaging in a conversation with this person, articulating your feelings and thoughts in a way you haven't managed or been able to in reality. Such dream encounters can range from heartfelt discussions to symbolic gestures of reconciliation. Upon waking, these dream experiences often leave you with a sense of resolution, as if a weight has been lifted off your shoulders. The impact of these dreams can be profound. They offer a sense of closure and understanding that, for various reasons, might be unattainable in your real-life interactions. This can be especially therapeutic in situations where the other person is no longer present in your life due to distance, estrangement, or even death. In this unique dreamscape, you are afforded the opportunity to process unresolved emotions, say the unspoken, and mend the emotional rifts, contributing significantly to your journey of emotional healing and closure.

Dreams Reflecting Emotional Growth

As we traverse through our emotional development, our dreams dynamically mirror this evolution, adapting and changing in tandem with our inner growth. This fascinating journey is evident in the progression of our dreams over time, which can serve as a reflective diary of our emotional and psychological states. Let's consider a scenario where you're grappling with personal insecurities or self-doubt in your waking life. Initially, your dreams might portray you as hesitant or passive, echoing your real-life challenges. However, as you consciously work on these insecurities, perhaps through therapy, self-reflection, or personal development efforts, a transformation gradually begins to unfold in your dream world. You might start to notice your dream-self exhibiting qualities of confidence and assertiveness, taking charge in situations that previously would have caused anxiety or hesitation. These changes in your dreams are not mere coincidences; they are profound indications of your emotional and psychological growth. The evolving nature of your dream-self becomes a symbolic representation of your newfound self-esteem and inner strength. This shift highlights the deep connection between our waking experiences and our subconscious expressions in dreams, demonstrating how dreams can not only reflect our current emotional state but also our journey of growth, healing, and self-realization.

Dreams and the Processing of Joyful Emotions
In the discourse surrounding dreams and their interpretation, there is often a significant emphasis on how they help us navigate and process negative emotions. However, it's equally important to acknowledge and appreciate the role of dreams in highlighting and enriching positive emotional experiences. Imagine dreams where you are at the heart of joyous celebrations, achieving long-sought goals, or reuniting with loved ones in scenarios filled with warmth and affection. These dreams do much more than merely replicate happy moments; they amplify and extend the feelings of happiness, love, and contentment into your waking life. They act as reminders of the positivity and joy that permeate your existence, sometimes overlooked in the hustle of everyday routines. Such dreams can have a reinforcing effect, cementing these positive emotions and experiences within your psyche. They serve as a counterbalance to the challenges of life,

offering a glimpse into the moments of sheer joy and fulfillment that are as much a part of life as its trials and tribulations. By celebrating your achievements, cherishing moments of happiness, and savoring feelings of love and connection in your dreams, you are reminded of the capacity for joy and positivity inherent in your life, thereby nurturing an overall sense of well-being and satisfaction.

Dreams are not just nightly escapades but potent tools for emotional exploration and healing. They act as a prism, revealing the multifaceted nature of our inner emotional landscape. Through our dreams, we engage in a dialogue with our deepest selves – confronting hidden fears, reveling in unacknowledged joys, and navigating the complexities of our emotional experiences. Dreams allow us to process emotions in a way that our waking consciousness may not always permit, offering a safe haven for expression, resolution, and understanding. By attentively observing and reflecting upon the narratives and emotions that our dreams present, we uncover invaluable insights about our emotional well-being. These insights can lead to the resolution of lingering emotional issues and aid in celebrating our emotional strengths and triumphs. The dream world, with all its mystery and complexity, is an integral part of our emotional tapestry, providing guidance and illumination as we journey through life. It encourages us to delve deeper into the understanding of our emotional selves, enriching our experience of life with greater awareness and empathy. In essence, dreams are a vital conduit to self-discovery and emotional well-being, bridging our conscious and subconscious worlds in a continuous dance of emotional exploration and growth.

Personal Dream Journeys

Do you recall the dream you had last night, or perhaps the one from the night before? Take a moment to think about how it made you feel. Every dream that visits us in the quiet of the night is more than just a fleeting series of images; it's a deeply personal narrative, an epic woven with rich symbolism and profound meaning. These dreams offer us invaluable insights into our deepest fears, our most cherished desires, and the values we hold dear. Picture yourself gently unraveling the intricate threads of your dreams, each one leading you to uncover hidden aspects of your personality, to decode the unspoken desires of your heart, or to bravely face the fears that murmur in the stillness of the night. This journey into the world of "Personal Dream Journeys" is a call to awaken your curiosity and venture into the enigmatic realm of your own dream world. It promises to be an illuminating expedition, one where each dream is a chapter in the unique and ongoing story of your life, revealing the diverse and complex nature of your personal journey. Let's embark on this adventure together, with a spirit of wonder and inquiry, ready to delve deep into the fascinating depths of our dreaming selves.

The Tapestry of Individual Experiences

Have you ever considered that your dreams are like a tapestry, intricately woven from the threads of your daily life? Think about it — every experience you have, every memory you cherish, and every emotion you feel, all these elements come together to create the vivid and complex dreams that you experience each night. For example, if you're a student, you might often find yourself dreaming about exams or sitting in classrooms. These dreams are reflecting the stress and pressures you face in your academic life. Or, if you've recently become a parent, don't be surprised if your dreams are filled with images of caring for a child or protecting them. It's fascinating, isn't it? How our dreams are so deeply personal and uniquely ours, colored by the very experiences and emotions that make up our waking lives. They're like our subconscious mind's way of processing and making sense of our daily experiences. So, the next time you dream, take a moment to think about what aspects of your life might be weaving themselves into the narrative of your dreams.

Dreams as Reflections of Personal Growth

Isn't it incredible how our dreams change and grow just as we do? Think back to the dreams you had as a child — they were probably full of fantasy, simple fears, maybe even magical adventures. Now, as an adult, your dreams might have evolved into more complex stories, haven't they? They often mirror the worries, hopes, and experiences that fill your day-to-day life. And you know, if you've ever faced and overcome big challenges in your life, it's likely that your dreams have reflected that journey too. They might have shifted from showing you struggling or feeling lost to scenarios where you come out on top, where you're the hero of your story. That's your mind celebrating your growth and resilience. It's fascinating how our subconscious keeps pace with our life's journey, adapting our dreams to mirror who we are and what we've been through. So, next time you wake up from a vivid dream, take a moment to think about what it might be telling you about your own personal growth.

Cultural and Familial Influences

Have you ever thought about how much your cultural background and family life influence your dreams? It's quite fascinating when you think about it. Our dreams often weave in aspects of our culture, traditions, and family stories, creating a unique language that's deeply personal to our heritage and upbringing. For example, if you grew up in a coastal community, don't be surprised if you find your dreams often filled with the ocean, waves, and beaches — these images are part of your subconscious tapestry. Or, let's say you come from a family of musicians. In that case, you might often dream about music, finding yourself in grand concert halls or hearing melodies that seem to create themselves. It's like our dreams are a reflection of where we come from and the environments that shaped us. They carry the imprints of our personal histories and backgrounds, painting dreamscapes that are as unique as our own life stories. Next time you dream, try to notice any elements that might be tied to your cultural or familial background. It's a little like being a detective in your own mind!

Emotional Processing in Dreams

Have you ever considered that our dreams are much more than just a replay of our daily lives? They're actually a kind of emotional processing center. Think about it — in our dreams, we get to rehearse for real-life situations, express emotions we might keep bottled up when we're awake, and even work through problems. It's like our own private laboratory for personal growth. Take, for example, dreaming about standing up to a bully. This isn't just a random dream; it's your subconscious preparing you, emotionally gearing you up to face similar challenges in your waking life. In this safe, dream space, you can confront fears, practice assertiveness, or find creative solutions to problems without any real-world risks. It's fascinating, isn't it, how our dreams can be such powerful tools for emotional readiness and resilience? So next time you have a particularly vivid dream, consider what it might be helping you to work through or prepare for. Your dreams might be training you for the challenges of your waking world!

Healing and Therapeutic Aspects

Did you know that for many people, dreams can be incredibly therapeutic, almost like a balm for the soul? It's true. Especially during those tough times — you know, when we're dealing with loss, or we're just feeling all mixed up inside — our dreams can offer a kind of comfort that's hard to find elsewhere. Let's say you're grieving the loss of someone close to you. It's a tough journey, isn't it? But then, you dream of that person. In your dream, they might be there with you, just like old times, and it feels so real, so comforting. It's almost as if through that dream, you're able to reconnect with them, find a sense of closeness that you're missing. This can be incredibly soothing and can help a lot in the healing process. Dreams have this unique way of offering clarity in our most confused moments and solace when we're in the midst of emotional chaos. So, if you ever find yourself waking up from a dream that's touched you deeply, know that it might be your mind's way of helping you heal, of giving you the comfort or the answers you need at that moment.

Dreams as a Mirror of Personal Challenges

You know, it's quite common for our dreams to mirror the challenges and dilemmas we face in our everyday lives. Picture yourself, for instance, caught up in the throes of making tough career decisions. It's a bit of a rollercoaster, right? Now, imagine how this stress and uncertainty might seep into your dreams. You might find yourself dreaming about standing at a crossroads or wandering through a complex labyrinth. These aren't just random dream settings; they're powerful symbols of the choices you're grappling with and your search for the right path in your professional life. Similarly, think about someone going through a rough patch in their relationship. They might dream about being separated from their partner or embarking on a solo journey. These dreams can be a reflection of what's going on deep down in their subconscious — a way of processing feelings of disconnect or the emotional distance they're experiencing. It's fascinating, isn't it, how our dreams can be such accurate reflections of our waking life challenges? They give us a glimpse into what's really bothering us, sometimes even before we're fully aware of it ourselves.

Symbolism Unique to the Individual

Have you ever noticed how the symbols in our dreams are so deeply personal, almost as if they've been custom-made just for us? Let me give you an example. Think about something special from your childhood, maybe a toy or a family heirloom. Now, imagine that object showing up in one of your dreams. It's not just there by chance; it's there for a reason. That object carries a whole world of personal meaning and emotions with it. Maybe it represents a happy memory, a sense of nostalgia, or perhaps something more complex that you haven't quite figured out yet. These symbols in our dreams, they're like keys that can unlock deeper emotional layers within us. They help us to unearth those undercurrents of feelings and maybe even unresolved issues from our past that we're not consciously aware of. It's pretty amazing when you think about it, how our minds use these familiar symbols to communicate with us, to help us understand ourselves better.

Recurring Dreams and Personal Themes

Do you ever have those dreams that keep coming back, night after night? They're quite intriguing, aren't they? Many of us experience these recurring dreams, and they usually have something important to tell us. Take, for instance, if you often find yourself dreaming about missing a flight. It's not just about the frustration of missing a plane; it could be pointing to a deeper fear in your waking life. Maybe it's about missing out on key opportunities or feeling like you're not quite prepared for the important things happening around you. When we have these recurring dreams, they're like little clues left by our subconscious, trying to tell us to pay attention to certain areas of our lives. Recognizing these patterns in our dreams, understanding what they mean, can be a real game-changer. It can help us address whatever underlying issues or concerns they're pointing towards. So, next time you find yourself in a familiar dream scenario, take a moment to reflect on what it might be trying to tell you about your life.

The Role of Fantasy and Wish Fulfillment

Isn't it amazing how our dreams can be like a playground for our wildest fantasies and deepest wishes? It's like, in our dreams, we can live out scenarios that we might never get to experience in our real lives. Imagine dreaming about climbing the highest mountain or being celebrated for a grand achievement — things that might feel out of reach in your day-to-day life. Or, picture revisiting a cherished memory, maybe a happy moment from your childhood or a special time with a loved one who's no longer with us. These dreams are more than just idle fantasies; they're a vital emotional outlet. They offer us comfort, help us to keep our hopes and aspirations alive, and sometimes, they can even motivate us to strive for more in our waking lives. By providing this balance, dreams allow us to escape, even if just for a little while, from the demands and limitations of daily life into the limitless realm of imagination. Next time you wake up from a dream where you've just done something incredible or revisited a precious moment, savor it! It's a beautiful gift from your subconscious, reminding you of the joys and possibilities life holds.

Dreams as a Reflection of Personal Relationships

Have you ever noticed how the people who populate our waking lives often make guest appearances in our dreams too? It's fascinating how our dreams weave in everyone from our closest loved ones to people we barely know. And the way they show up in our dreams, the roles they play, it's all very telling. For instance, think about a dream where you're just laughing and having a great time with a friend. That dream could be reflecting the strong, positive bond you share with them. But then, there are those dreams where you might be arguing with a family member. These aren't just random narratives; they could be signaling some real-life tensions or unresolved issues that you might need to address. It's like our dreams are holding up a mirror to our relationships, showing us the true nature of our feelings and connections. So, next time you dream about someone you know, take a moment to think about what that dream might be saying about your relationship with them. It could be more insightful than you realize!

Each dream is a story, a piece of a much larger puzzle that makes up who you are. They're this unique blend of your deepest hopes, your most nagging fears, your cherished memories, and your wildest desires. All of these elements come together in the theater of your subconscious, creating scenes that can be both bewildering and enlightening. And when you take the time to really dive into these dreams, to ponder and reflect on them, you start to uncover layers of yourself you might not have known existed. You begin to understand not just your own inner workings, but also how you relate to others and your place in the larger world. These dream journeys, they're far from being just random thoughts or images; they're meaningful explorations of your psyche. They help you unravel the complex narrative of your life, revealing the beauty, the struggles, and everything in between. So, the next time you wake up from a vivid dream, consider it an invitation to explore and understand a little more about your own personal story.

CHAPTER ELEVEN

Interpreting Your Dreams

Have you ever thought of yourself as a detective, but instead of solving mysteries out in the world, you're unraveling the mysteries of your own mind? That's exactly what happens when you start interpreting your dreams. Each dream you have is like a puzzle, wrapped in the complex and often mysterious language of your subconscious. It's an intriguing process, isn't it? Together, let's dive into this fascinating journey. We'll look at the symbols, the emotions, and the narratives your dreams present. Think of it as piecing together clues to understand the deeper messages your mind is trying to communicate. You know, the things you might not be fully aware of when you're awake. Whether it's a recurring dream that's been puzzling you or a bizarre dream that left you bewildered when you woke up, there's always something to uncover. So, are you ready to play detective and explore the hidden realms of your dreams?

The Art of Dream Interpretation
Think of dream interpretation as a beautiful blend of art and insight, where your intuition meets your

understanding. It's kind of like being an explorer, isn't it? You look beyond just what's happening on the surface of your dreams and dive deeper into what these symbols might really mean. Take flying in a dream, for example. You might initially think it's just about the thrill of soaring high in the sky, but it could be tapping into something deeper, like your longing for freedom, your high-reaching ambitions, or maybe a deep-seated desire to break free from something in your life. So, when you're trying to figure out your dreams, keep an open mind, be willing to think outside the box, and explore all the different angles and possibilities. Each dream is a unique and intriguing puzzle, just waiting for you to unlock its secrets.

Personal Symbols and Meanings

Let's talk about one of the most fascinating aspects of dream interpretation — understanding that the symbols in your dreams are incredibly personal to you. It's like they have your own secret code. What a symbol means in your dream could be completely different from what it means in someone else's. It all comes down to your unique life experiences, your individual fears, and even your hopes and dreams. For instance, think about how a childhood toy might show up in your dream. To one person, that toy might bring back warm, nostalgic feelings, a reminder of carefree days. But for someone else, the same toy could represent something they've lost or left behind, maybe a sense of innocence or a part of their life that's no longer there. This is what makes dream interpretation so personal and so intriguing. Your dreams are a reflection of your inner world, painted with symbols that speak directly to you and your experiences.

Emotional Context of Dreams

Here's something I'd love for you to consider: the emotions you feel in a dream are often as crucial as the dream itself. It's like your subconscious is speaking to you through feelings. Next time you have a dream, try to remember not just what you saw, but how you felt. Was there anxiety, fear, joy, or freedom? These emotions can be powerful indicators. For example, if you wake up from a dream feeling anxious or scared, it might be your mind's way of pointing out areas in your waking life where you're feeling a bit lost or out of control. On the flip side, if you experience a dream where you're overflowing with joy or feeling incredibly free, it could be reflecting something really positive in your life, like a recent achievement or a newfound sense of confidence. It's fascinating, isn't it, how our dreams can give us such insight into our emotions? They're like a window into our deeper selves, helping us to understand our feelings and reactions to the world around us.

Recurring Dreams and Patterns

Have you ever experienced dreams that keep coming back, night after night? It's quite intriguing, right? I want you to consider something important about these recurring dreams. They're not just random; they're like signals from your subconscious, trying to catch your attention. Think of them as your mind's way of saying, 'Hey, there's something here you need to look at.' These repeated dreams often point to unresolved issues or life lessons that you're maybe not addressing during your waking hours. So, next time you notice a recurring dream, try to see the pattern. What is the common theme or the recurring situation? Understanding these patterns can give you some really valuable insights into challenges or issues that keep cropping up in your life. It's like your dreams are giving you clues, helping you to piece together a puzzle that your subconscious is urgently trying to solve.

Dream Journals: A Tool for Interpretation

You know, one of the best tools you can have on your journey to understanding your dreams is a dream journal. Think of it as your personal dream detective notebook. Here's what I suggest: as soon as you wake up, grab your journal and jot down everything you can remember about your dreams. It might seem a bit fuzzy at first, but you'd be surprised at how much comes back to you once you start writing. The more details, the better — the colors, the feelings, the people, everything. Over time, this journal becomes like a treasure trove of insights. You can look back and start to see patterns, recurring symbols, or emotional themes. It's like putting together pieces of a puzzle. This practice can really open up your understanding of your dreams, and in turn, give you a clearer picture of what's going on in your subconscious mind. Plus, it's pretty fascinating to see how your dream world evolves over time!

Seeking External Perspectives

Have you ever thought about sharing your dreams with others? Sometimes, getting a different perspective can be really eye-opening. Next time you have a particularly vivid or puzzling dream, why not share it with a friend or a family member? You'd be surprised at how different people can offer fresh insights or interpretations you might not have considered. And if you're really keen on diving deep, you might even think about chatting with someone who specializes in dream interpretation. They can bring a whole new level of understanding to what your subconscious might be trying to communicate. It's like looking at your dream through a different lens, and suddenly, things that seemed confusing or unclear start to make sense. Plus, it's a great way to connect with others and share a bit of the mysterious world of your dreams. You never know what new understanding a fresh set of eyes (or ears) can bring to your dream experience!

Recognizing Universal Symbols
Did you know that while interpreting your dreams is a very personal journey, there are actually some symbols that a lot of us dream about? These are like universal dream symbols. Take water, for example. It's a common dream symbol that usually has to do with emotions. The state of the water in your dream can tell you a lot about your emotional state. Calm, clear water might suggest you're feeling emotionally balanced, while turbulent, murky water could indicate emotional upheaval or confusion. Recognizing these universal symbols can be a great starting point for understanding your dreams. But here's the catch — it's crucial to relate these symbols back to your own life. Think about what water means to you personally. Maybe you have a specific memory or feeling tied to it. Connecting these universal symbols to your personal experiences and emotions is where the real magic of dream interpretation happens. It's like piecing together a puzzle that's all about you and your inner world.

The Role of Culture in Dream Interpretation
Have you ever considered how much your cultural background shapes the way you interpret your dreams? It's

really quite fascinating. You see, across different cultures, the same symbol in a dream can mean entirely different things. Let's take the example of a snake. In some cultures, dreaming about a snake might set off alarm bells; it could symbolize danger or deceit. But in other cultures, a snake in a dream could be a positive sign, representing healing, transformation, or even spiritual awakening. So when you're trying to figure out what your dreams might be telling you, it's really important to think about the cultural lens you're looking through. Your personal and cultural background can play a huge role in shaping how you interpret the symbols and themes in your dreams. It's like each culture has its own dream language, and understanding that can really enrich your perspective on what your dreams are communicating.

Dreams as a Reflection of Your Daily Life

Have you ever noticed how what happens during your day can find its way into your dreams at night? It's like your daily experiences are setting the stage for the night's dream theater. For instance, if you're going through a particularly stressful time, you might find that your dreams become more intense, maybe even a bit chaotic. It's your mind's way of processing all that stress. On the other hand, when you're having a period of peace and happiness, your dreams often reflect that too, leading to more pleasant or uplifting dream scenarios. So, whenever you have a memorable dream, take a moment to think about what's been happening in your life recently. Understanding this connection can give you some pretty interesting insights into how your subconscious mind is dealing with your waking life. It's like your dreams are giving you clues about what's really going on inside your head.

The Significance of Characters in Dreams
Isn't it interesting how the people in our dreams, whether they're familiar faces or complete strangers, can carry so much meaning? It's like each person who shows up in your dream has a role to play in the story of your subconscious. Think about it — the people in your dreams might be representing different aspects of your own self or mirroring the dynamics of your relationships in real life. For example, a friend appearing in your dream could actually be reflecting a part of your personality that's similar to them. Or maybe a stranger in your dream is showing you a perspective or an aspect of life that you're not familiar with. It's worth pondering over the characters in your dreams and the roles they play. Are they guiding you, challenging you, or maybe showing you something about yourself? Understanding this can give you a deeper insight into your own psyche and how you interact with the world around you.

Interpreting Abstract and Complex Dreams
Have you ever woken up from a dream that felt like a straightforward story, and then, other times, from dreams that are just so abstract and complex they feel like a puzzle? It's pretty common, you know. When you have those complex, intricate dreams, it's helpful to break them down a bit. Think about dissecting them into different elements and themes, sort of like analyzing a piece of art. What's the overarching narrative? What feelings does it stir up in you? It's okay if these abstract dreams don't make immediate sense or have a clear-cut interpretation. Sometimes, they're not meant to be fully unraveled. Even in their complexity and ambiguity, they can shed light on the inner workings

of your subconscious mind. These dreams can offer you glimpses, however cryptic, into your deeper self, your fears, your desires, and more. So, the next time you find yourself puzzled by a dream, remember, it's another piece of the fascinating puzzle that is your mind.

Intuition and Dream Interpretation

You know, when it comes to interpreting your dreams, one of the best pieces of advice I can give you is to trust your intuition. It's like having an inner guide. You might read about traditional meanings of dream symbols, but sometimes they just don't click, and that's okay. Have you ever had a dream and, despite what the dream dictionaries say, you just feel in your gut that it means something else? That's your intuition speaking, and it's often pretty spot on. Your personal connection to a dream, how it makes you feel, and what it stirs up inside you — that's a powerful tool for understanding what your subconscious is trying to tell you. It's like your own internal language of symbols and emotions. So next time you're puzzling over a dream, take a moment to tune into what your instincts are telling you about it. More often than not, your gut feeling will lead you to a deeper understanding of your dream's message.

Dream Interpretation as a Journey, Not a Destination

Before we wrap up, there's something important I'd like you to keep in mind about interpreting your dreams: it's all about the journey, not the destination. Dream interpretation isn't something you master overnight, and it's not about finding definitive answers to each dream. It's an ongoing process, a path of exploration and discovery. As you grow and change, your understanding of your dreams will evolve too. You'll start seeing your dreams in new lights, uncovering different layers of meaning as you move through different stages of your life. This evolving nature of dream interpretation is what makes it so exciting and deeply personal. So, embrace this journey with an open heart. Enjoy each insight, each revelation about yourself that comes from understanding your dreams. It's a fascinating adventure into your inner world, one that offers endless opportunities for self-discovery and growth.

So, as we come to the end of our chat about dreams, I want you to remember that interpreting your dreams is a very personal and unique journey. It's about blending a bit of everything – understanding those universal symbols that pop up in dreams, acknowledging how your own culture shapes your dream narratives, reflecting on what's happening in your everyday life, and seeing how all of that plays out in the characters and scenarios of your dreams. And don't forget the most important part – trusting your gut. Your intuition is a powerful guide when it comes to understanding what your dreams are trying to tell you. Keep in mind that as you grow and change, so will your dreams and their meanings. Embracing this ever-evolving process is what makes dream interpretation so fascinating. As you continue to explore the world of your dreams, you'll find that you're not just uncovering the mysteries of your subconscious mind; you're also gaining a richer, deeper understanding of the story of your life.

CHAPTER TWELVE

Historical Theories of Dream Interpretation

Have you ever wondered about the journey we've taken as humans to understand our dreams? It's a story that spans throughout history, and it's absolutely fascinating. Let's go on a little time travel together and explore some of the key theories that have shaped how we think about dreams. From ancient civilizations who saw dreams as divine messages to the groundbreaking psychoanalytic theories of Freud and Jung, each era has had its own take on what dreams mean. It's like each period in history added a new piece to the puzzle of understanding our dreams. So, as we embark on this journey, think about how these historical perspectives might have influenced the way you view your own dreams today. It's a rich tapestry of beliefs and theories, each offering a unique insight into the mysterious world of dreaming.

Ancient Civilizations: Dreams as Divine Messages
Let's turn the clock way back and start with how people in ancient times viewed dreams. It's really interesting. Back then, dreams were often seen as more than just night-time stories; they were messages from the gods or the spiritual

realm. Take the ancient Egyptians, for instance. They truly believed that dreams were a way the gods communicated with them. They even had professional 'dream interpreters' — kind of like the ancient version of a psychologist, right? And then there were the ancient Greeks. They took dreams pretty seriously too. They believed dreams had prophetic powers and could foretell the future. The Greeks even built temples dedicated to their god of healing, Asclepius, where people would go to sleep and receive healing dreams sent by the gods. Can you imagine that? Going to sleep in a temple, hoping to receive a dream that could cure you? It's fascinating how much weight and significance was placed on dreams in these ancient cultures.

Biblical Perspectives: Visions and Prophecies

Have you ever thought about the role dreams play in the Bible? It's quite remarkable. In the Bible, dreams are often portrayed as a way God communicates with people. A famous example is Joseph from the Old Testament — remember how he interpreted Pharaoh's dreams? It's a fascinating story. Joseph's ability to understand these divine messages not only saved Egypt from famine but also elevated his own status. These biblical dreams weren't just regular night visions; they were seen as prophetic, providing guidance, warnings, or even foreshadowing future events. It kind of makes you wonder about the deeper meanings and messages that could be hidden in our own dreams, doesn't it? The idea that dreams could be a conduit for divine communication is a powerful one and has influenced the way many people view their dreams even today.

Aristotle's Naturalistic View

Let's talk about Aristotle for a moment. He was this brilliant ancient Greek philosopher, and his take on dreams was pretty ahead of his time. Unlike many of his contemporaries who viewed dreams as divine or prophetic, Aristotle had a different angle. He suggested that dreams were actually the result of sensory impressions we pick up during the day. So, in his view, when we dream, it's not some mystical experience; it's our mind's way of processing and making sense of our daily experiences. It's like our brain is doing a bit of housekeeping while we sleep, sorting through all the sights, sounds, and feelings we encountered throughout the day. Aristotle's naturalistic approach to dreams was a big shift from the more supernatural interpretations of his time, and it really paved the way for future scientific exploration into why we dream. Kind of fascinating, don't you think?

Freud's Psychoanalytic Theory

Jumping forward to the late 19th and early 20th centuries, let's chat about Sigmund Freud, a name you've probably heard before. He was this revolutionary thinker who really changed the game in how we understand dreams. Freud came up with psychoanalytic theory, and he saw dreams as a window into our deepest desires and anxieties, stuff that's often tucked away in our subconscious. He believed many of these hidden emotions are tied to our childhood experiences or even to our sexual desires. It was pretty controversial stuff at the time! He wrote this book called 'The Interpretation of Dreams,' and let me tell you, it's a foundational work in the world of dream analysis. Freud's ideas opened up a whole new way of looking at dreams, not just as random images and thoughts, but as meaningful reflections of our innermost psyche. His work laid the groundwork for pretty much all modern dream interpretation. Pretty incredible, right?

Carl Jung's Collective Unconscious

Now, let's talk about Carl Jung. He was a student of Freud, but he took dream interpretation in a slightly different direction. Jung was really fascinated by the symbolic side of dreams. He came up with this idea of the 'collective unconscious,' which is like a pool of shared memories and ideas that all of us, as humans, have access to. According to Jung, our dreams dip into this collective unconscious and bring up all these symbols that are packed with meaning. He believed that by interpreting these symbols, we can uncover a lot about our personal growth and our inner psyche. It's like each dream is a piece of a puzzle, and when you start putting these pieces together, you get a clearer picture of who you are and what's going on beneath the surface. Jung's approach really highlights the depth and complexity of our dreams, showing us that they're not just random thoughts, but gateways to understanding deeper aspects of ourselves and our shared human experience.

Modern Theories: Neurobiological Perspectives

Let's fast forward to the present day and take a look at how the field of neurobiology is changing our understanding of dreams. It's quite a leap from the days of Freud and Jung! Nowadays, scientists are delving into how our brains work when we're dreaming, and what they're finding is super interesting. Modern theories suggest that dreaming isn't just about unpacking our subconscious thoughts or desires; it's actually a cognitive process. This process plays a big role in how we consolidate our memories and work through our emotions. Researchers are now studying brain activity during sleep, using all this high-tech equipment to get a glimpse into what happens in our minds when we dream. It's like they're unlocking the scientific side of our dream world, trying to understand not just why we dream, but how dreaming affects our brain's functioning. This neurobiological perspective is adding a whole new dimension to dream interpretation, bridging the gap between the psychological and the physiological. It's a fascinating time to be exploring the world of dreams!

The Enlightenment and Rationalism

Now, let's zoom into the Enlightenment era, a time when the way people thought about dreams started to change quite a bit. This was when rationalism was all the rage. People started looking at dreams in a completely different light. Instead of seeing them as mystical messages or supernatural signs, dreams began to be viewed as just byproducts of our restless minds. It was quite the shift! The mysticism that surrounded dreams kind of took a backseat, and a more scientific, psychological approach started to emerge. Think about philosophers like Descartes and Hobbes – they saw dreams as pretty inconsequential, just the result of random brain activity firing off while we sleep. It's fascinating, isn't it, how the cultural and intellectual climate of an era can so significantly influence how we interpret something as personal as our dreams?

Romanticism and the Subconscious

Let's swing the pendulum to the Romantic period, which painted a starkly different picture of dreams compared to the rationalists of the Enlightenment. This was a time when fascination with dreams made a big comeback. The Romantics, like Samuel Taylor Coleridge and William Blake, they really embraced dreams as these profound gateways to the subconscious mind. For them, dreams weren't just random brain firings; they were like portals to the deeper, mystical parts of our psyche. Imagine being a poet or an artist in that era, drawing inspiration from the vivid, symbolic dreamscapes that visit you at night. That's exactly what many Romantics did. They reignited the idea that dreams are more than just nighttime experiences; they're bridges to a deeper understanding of ourselves and our human experience. It was a time when dreams regained their status as powerful sources of insight and creativity.

The Influence of Eastern Philosophies

You know, as Western ideas about dreams evolved, there was also this growing curiosity about how Eastern philosophies view dreams. It's like opening a whole new door to understanding our dream world. Take Hindu and Buddhist traditions, for example. They have this fascinating view of dreams as illusions, or 'Maya,' as they call it. In these traditions, dreams are seen as reflections of our desires and attachments, the kind of stuff that can cloud our understanding of reality. It's a perspective that adds a whole new layer to dream interpretation. Instead of just looking at dreams as messages or psychological processes, these Eastern philosophies bring in the idea of the spiritual journey. Dreams, in this view, are part of the path toward enlightenment and self-realization. It's like they're tools to help us see beyond the superficial aspects of life and understand the deeper truths about ourselves and the world. Quite a shift from how we usually think about dreams, right?

Freud vs. Jung: A Divergence in Psychoanalysis
Let's talk about a really interesting chapter in the history of dream interpretation: the split between Freud and Jung's theories. It's like a fork in the road for understanding dreams. Freud, whom we talked about earlier, he really honed in on dreams as outlets for our repressed desires and unresolved childhood conflicts. His view was all about the personal, hidden stuff bubbling under the surface. But then, there's Carl Jung, who took a different path. Jung looked at dreams through a broader, more holistic lens. He wasn't just interested in personal experiences; he delved into what he called archetypes and the collective unconscious. This means he thought our dreams tapped into something much bigger — shared symbols and myths that span across cultures and time. It's a fascinating contrast, isn't it? While Freud focused on the individual psyche, Jung opened the door to a world of universal symbols and deeper meanings in our dreams. Their differing perspectives really expanded the way we can interpret our nighttime stories.

Contemporary Approaches: From Science to Spirituality
Now, fast forward to the modern era, and you'll see that the way we interpret dreams has become incredibly diverse and multi-layered. Today, it's not just about one school of thought; we're combining insights from psychology, neuroscience, and even spirituality to understand our dreams. Contemporary psychologists and neuroscientists are doing some really cool stuff, like diving into how our brains work when we dream and what that can tell us about our cognitive processes and mental health. But that's not all — alongside all this scientific exploration, there's also been a kind of revival in looking at dreams through a more

spiritual and mystical lens, kind of circling back to the ancient belief in the deeper significance of dreams. It's like we're now looking at dreams from every angle possible, blending the old with the new, to understand not just what we dream, but why we dream and how it connects us to something bigger than ourselves. It's a fascinating time to be delving into the world of dreams, don't you think?

The Multidisciplinary Approach

Isn't it amazing how, in today's world, understanding our dreams has become this incredible collaborative effort across different fields? Think of it like a team of experts from all walks of life coming together to decipher the mysteries of our dreams. You have psychologists, neuroscientists, anthropologists, and even spiritual leaders, all adding their unique perspectives. It's no longer just about one way of seeing things; it's this rich, multidimensional exploration. Psychologists might dive into what your dreams say about your personal psyche, while neuroscientists could look at what's happening in your brain as you dream. Anthropologists might explore how dreams fit into different cultures, and spiritual leaders might offer insights into the more mystical aspects of dreaming. This whole integrative approach has opened up so many more avenues to understand not just what we dream about, but why we dream and how these dreams connect us to the larger tapestry of human experience. It's like piecing together a giant puzzle where each piece comes from a different discipline, giving us a much more nuanced and comprehensive picture of our dream world.

As we wrap up our journey through the history of dream interpretation, it's incredible to think about how this quest reflects our endless curiosity about the human mind and our own experiences. From the ancient civilizations that viewed dreams as divine messages, all the way to modern scientists unraveling the mysteries of the brain, every step in this journey tells a story about us – about humanity's unending quest for knowledge and understanding of the self. Every theory, every perspective from history, has layered more depth and richness into how we understand dreams. It's a field that's as old as time, yet it's always evolving, always offering new insights and new mysteries to explore. This journey through the history of dreams is a clear reminder of how our quest to understand our dreams is deeply intertwined with our quest to understand ourselves. And that's what makes it an endlessly fascinating area, not just for study, but for personal reflection, don't you think?

CHAPTER THIRTEEN

Therapeutic Uses of Dream Interpretation

Isn't it amazing how dream interpretation has carved out such a significant role in therapy? It's like we've discovered a unique path that leads straight to personal growth and emotional healing. Think of it this way: when we dive into understanding our dreams, we're not just indulging in a bit of curiosity; we're actually engaging in a powerful therapeutic process. By exploring our dreams, we can get a better grasp of who we are, how we interact with others, and even enhance our interpersonal skills. It's like each dream is a piece of a puzzle that, when put together, reveals a bigger picture of our inner world. And there's more — dream interpretation can be a great tool for coping with life's challenges. Our dreams often hold the keys to our deepest emotions and unresolved issues. By interpreting these dreams, we can uncover hidden parts of ourselves, understand our fears and desires, and work towards healing. It's like embarking on a journey of self-discovery, where each dream is a step towards understanding more about who we are and how we can grow. So, as we explore this fascinating world of dream interpretation together, think of it as a tool, not just for insight, but for profound emotional and personal development.

Uncovering the Unconscious

Have you ever considered that your dreams could be a direct line to your unconscious mind? It's like they're a secret tunnel to the thoughts, fears, and desires you might not even realize you have. Picture this: therapists often use dream analysis as a tool to help their clients dig into these hidden corners of their psyche. It's kind of like a detective piecing together clues. For example, imagine you have a recurring dream where you're speaking in front of a huge crowd and suddenly you're voiceless. A therapist might help you explore this dream to uncover a deeper fear of not being heard or anxiety about public speaking. By delving into these dream scenarios, you can uncover a lot about what's bubbling under the surface of your conscious mind. This process of interpreting dreams can lead to some pretty eye-opening insights about your subconscious motivations and those emotional issues you haven't quite resolved yet. It's fascinating when you think about it, how much your dreams can tell you about yourself.

Processing Emotional Trauma

You know, for people who've gone through traumatic experiences, their dreams can often be a replay or reflection of those tough times. It's like their mind is trying to process what happened, even when they're asleep. In therapy, understanding and interpreting these dreams becomes a crucial part of the healing journey. Let me give you an example. Suppose someone's been through a really frightening car accident. They might have recurring dreams about cars, crashes, or even just the feeling of being out of control. In a therapeutic setting, a therapist would help them unpack these dreams. It's a way for the individual to safely explore and work through the emotions tied to their trauma — fear, helplessness, anxiety — all within a controlled and supportive environment. This process can be incredibly helpful in making sense of their traumatic experience and taking those first steps on the path to recovery. It's about giving the mind a space to heal and find closure, and often, that starts with understanding the stories and emotions that come up in our dreams.

Exploring Relationship Dynamics

Have you ever noticed how the people in your life often show up in your dreams? It's like our minds are using these dreams to tell us something about our relationships. For instance, let's say you dream about a colleague. In the dream, you might be working together seamlessly, which could reflect a positive real-life working relationship. Or maybe you're arguing in the dream, which could be your subconscious picking up on some underlying tension. In therapy, digging into these representations can be really eye-opening. A therapist can help you understand why certain people appear in your dreams and what that says about your relationship with them. This can be super helpful for working through conflicts or misunderstandings you might have in your waking life. It's like your dreams are giving you clues about how to improve your relationships, understand your emotional needs better, and develop healthier ways of relating to the people around you. So next time someone you know pops up in a dream, it might be worth thinking about what your dream is trying to tell you about your connection with them.

Facilitating Personal Growth

Let's chat about how dream interpretation isn't just for understanding your subconscious, but it can also be a fantastic tool for your personal growth. When you start to interpret your dreams, it's like you're embarking on a journey of introspection and self-reflection. For instance, imagine you have a dream where you're climbing a mountain, but you keep slipping. This could symbolize challenges you're facing in achieving a goal in your waking life. Now, in therapy, a therapist can help you explore this dream, leading to some real 'aha' moments about your life path, your goals, and what's holding you back. They can even guide you to use this dream as a source of inspiration — maybe it's telling you to persevere or find new ways to tackle challenges. This process can be incredibly motivating, helping you to not just understand your dreams but also to use them as a springboard to work towards your personal goals and aspirations. So, you see, your dreams can actually be a treasure trove of insights and inspiration for your personal growth journey!

Confronting Fears and Anxieties

Did you know that our dreams can be like a mirror, reflecting our deepest fears and anxieties? It's pretty fascinating. In therapy, understanding and confronting these fearful aspects of our dreams can be a real game-changer. Imagine you frequently have dreams where you're being chased. This could be your subconscious highlighting a fear or anxiety you're dealing with in your day-to-day life. Maybe it's a fear of failure or a sense of being overwhelmed. In a therapeutic setting, you get to explore these dreams in a safe and controlled way. It's like having a practice ground to face your fears, understand where they're coming from, and then work on strategies to tackle them in real life. This process can be incredibly empowering. By getting to the root of these fears in your dreams, you can start making changes to manage them, not just when you're asleep, but also in your waking life. It's all about taking those scary things in your dreams, understanding them, and then using that knowledge to empower yourself in the real world.

Enhancing Creativity and Problem-Solving

Have you ever thought of your dreams as a source of creativity, kind of like a spring that's always bubbling up with fresh, innovative ideas? It's true, you know. Dreams can be incredibly creative and can even offer us unconventional solutions to problems we face. In therapy, this aspect of dreams is sometimes used to spark creativity. For example, imagine you're an artist or a writer facing a block. A therapist might suggest looking into your dreams for inspiration. Maybe you dreamt of a bizarre, otherworldly landscape — that could become the setting for your next story or painting. Or let's say you're dealing with a tough problem at work. A solution might come to you in a dream, in a way you'd never consider while you're awake. It's because dreams have this unique way of bypassing our logical thinking and tapping into more creative parts of our brain. Therapists often encourage clients to explore their dreams, not just to understand them, but to use them as a tool for creative expression or to approach personal and professional challenges from a whole new angle.

As we wrap up our conversation on the therapeutic uses of dream interpretation, it's like we're closing a chapter in a book that's opened up a fascinating world of self-discovery and healing. Think of it as building a bridge between your conscious mind and the hidden depths of your unconscious. This bridge is built on insights from your dreams, and it can lead to some truly profound emotional and psychological growth. Studies have shown that engaging with our dreams can improve our problem-solving skills, reduce anxiety, and even enhance our creativity. It's not just about deciphering symbols; it's about tapping into a part of ourselves that we're often not fully aware of. By exploring our dreams, we get to understand ourselves on a deeper level. We uncover fears, desires, and motivations that we might not have been conscious of. And here's the really exciting part: this understanding can be the key to unlocking significant changes and improvements in our lives. Whether it's personal growth, overcoming emotional barriers, or just gaining a new perspective on life's challenges, dream interpretation offers a unique and powerful tool. So, as we close this chapter, remember that your dreams are more than just nighttime stories. They're a window into your inner world, offering a path to healing and growth that's as unique as you are.

CHAPTER FOURTEEN

Spiritual Aspects of Dreams in Hindu Philosophy

Did you know that in Hindu philosophy, dreams are seen as so much more than just something that happens when you sleep? They're considered deeply spiritual experiences, rich with meaning and insights. It's a perspective that opens up a whole new world when it comes to understanding dreams. Instead of just random thoughts or images, dreams in Hinduism are viewed as significant events that can offer profound understanding and guidance. In this chapter, we're going to dive into this fascinating perspective. We'll explore how Hinduism looks at the spiritual dimension of dreams, how these nightly experiences can be gateways to deeper truths, and what they can teach us about ourselves and the world around us. It's a journey into a realm where dreams are not just a part of our sleep but a vital part of our spiritual life. So, let's get started and see what these ancient wisdoms can reveal to us about the mysterious world of dreams

Dreams in Vedantic Thought

Let's take a closer look at Vedanta, which is a really important school of thought in Hindu philosophy, especially when it comes to understanding dreams. Vedanta teaches that there are different states of consciousness, and it places a lot of significance on dreams. According to the Mandukya Upanishad, a crucial text in Vedanta, we experience three states of consciousness: there's the waking state, which is called Jagrat; the dreaming state, known as Swapna; and then deep sleep, or Sushupti. But beyond these, there's an ultimate state called Turiya, the transcendental state. Now, in the context of dreams, or the Swapna state, it's really interesting because it's seen as a time when our soul is not bound by the physical world. It's like in our dreams, we're free to explore and gain insights into the true nature of reality and ourselves. Imagine dreaming about flying, for example. In Vedanta, this could be seen as an expression of the soul's freedom, unshackled from the physical limits of the waking world. It's a perspective that turns dreaming into a profound experience, offering us a glimpse into deeper truths about who we are and the nature of our existence.

Dreams as a Means to Self-Realization

Did you know that in Hindu philosophy, dreams are often seen as more than just random stories your mind tells at night? They're actually viewed as important tools for self-realization and spiritual growth. It's like when you're dreaming, you're receiving messages from the divine or your higher self. These messages are there to guide you on your spiritual journey. It's as if your dreams are a medium, revealing hidden truths and spiritual lessons that help you understand your path in life — your Dharma, which is your duty, and your Karma, the actions you take. For instance, if you have a dream where you're helping people, it could be a message about your Dharma, pointing you towards a path of service and kindness. These dreams can really help in making sense of your spiritual journey and guide you towards fulfilling your true purpose in life. It's fascinating how dreams can hold such deep spiritual significance in Hindu philosophy, isn't it?

Symbolism in Hindu Dream Interpretation

In Hinduism, dreams are like a canvas painted with all sorts of symbols and metaphors, each holding deep spiritual meanings. It's quite fascinating. You see, common symbols that pop up in dreams, like snakes, lotuses, or mountains, aren't just random images. They carry specific meanings that can shed light on your life and spiritual journey. Let's take the snake, for example. In many Hindu traditions, dreaming of a snake isn't something to fear. Instead, it's often seen as a symbol of Kundalini energy, which is a form of primal energy thought to be coiled at the base of the spine. So, dreaming of a snake could signify a spiritual awakening or a rise in consciousness. And what about mountains? They often symbolize the challenges or obstacles we face on our path to spiritual enlightenment. Imagine you're dreaming of climbing a steep mountain; it could reflect your personal struggles as you strive for higher spiritual understanding. It's really intriguing how these symbols in dreams can offer such profound insights into our spiritual lives, don't you think?

Dreams and Yoga Practices

Have you ever considered how dreams and yoga could be connected? Especially in certain Yoga practices, like Tantra and Kundalini Yoga, dreams play a really unique role. These traditions use dreams as a way to go beyond our usual, everyday consciousness. It's not just about physical poses; there are specific techniques in these forms of Yoga to actually control and understand dreams. Think of it as using your dreams as a tool to reach higher states of consciousness and, ultimately, spiritual enlightenment. For instance, in Kundalini Yoga, there's a focus on awakening the 'Kundalini energy,' which is believed to lie dormant at the base of the spine. Practitioners might find that as they advance in their practice, their dreams become more vivid or significant, offering insights or experiences that reflect their spiritual awakening. It's like their dream world becomes an extension of their yogic journey, providing a deeper understanding of themselves and the universe. Pretty fascinating, right? The way these practices intertwine with the world of dreams opens up a whole new dimension to both spiritual practice and dream interpretation.

The Role of Dreams in Hindu Mythology
Let's dive into the enchanting world of Hindu mythology, where dreams are not just nightly occurrences but pivotal elements in many stories. You see, in these ancient tales, gods and goddesses often communicate with mortals through their dreams. It's like their divine hotline! These dreams are ways for deities to impart wisdom, offer warnings, or even bestow blessings on humans. For example, there's a story where Lord Vishnu appears in King Muchukunda's dream to grant him a boon for his devotion. Or tales where dreams are used by the gods to guide and protect heroes on their epic quests. These stories from Hindu mythology aren't just fascinating tales; they deeply

reinforce the belief in the spiritual significance of dreams. They show how dreams can be profound, life-changing experiences, filled with divine messages and guidance. It's a perspective that really highlights the sacred and mystical dimensions of dreaming in Hindu culture.

Dreams and the Illusion of Maya

In Hindu philosophy, there's this fascinating concept of Maya, which basically means that the material world around us is an illusion. Now, think about how this concept applies to dreams. In this context, dreams are seen as a reflection of Maya, emphasizing that both our waking life and our dream state are, in a sense, illusory. It's like saying that what we experience in our daily lives and in our dreams might not be the ultimate reality. For example, you might dream of being a king or flying through the skies, but when you wake up, you realize it was just a dream. Similarly, Hindu philosophy suggests that our waking experiences could also be a kind of 'dream,' a temporary reality. This viewpoint really encourages us to look beyond the surface, beyond these illusory experiences, to seek a deeper, more profound truth about existence and the universe. It's a perspective that challenges us to question what we perceive as reality and to search for the ultimate truth that lies beyond the ordinary experiences of life and dreams.

As we wrap up our conversation about dreams in Hindu philosophy, it's really important to recognize that dreams are seen as so much more than just a play of the subconscious. In Hindu thought, they're integral to our spiritual awakening and journey toward self-realization. You see, the spiritual dimension of dreams in Hinduism isn't just a side aspect; it's central to understanding the nature of reality, our true self, and the ultimate truths of existence. It's like dreams are a window, offering us unique and profound insights that we might not easily access in our waking life. By exploring and understanding these spiritual aspects of dreams, we get to appreciate the mystical and transcendental elements that are so deeply woven into Hindu philosophy. It's an invitation to look deeper, beyond the surface of our nightly visions, to uncover insights and truths that can guide us on our spiritual path. So, when we consider our dreams through this lens, it's not just about interpreting symbols; it's about connecting with a deeper, more spiritual part of ourselves and the universe.

CHAPTER FIFTEEN

The Journey Continues

As we reach the final pages of "Dream Pilgrims - A Journey into the Subconscious," I feel we're parting ways at the end of a shared adventure. Together, we've traversed the intricate landscape of dreams, exploring their hidden crevices and soaring heights. But, as with all good journeys, the end is just another beginning.

Our exploration has taken us through Hindu philosophy's symbolic realms, psychoanalysis's analytical depths, and the shared experiences of global dream cultures. We've seen how dreams can be a mirror, a guide, and a source of creative inspiration. But remember, this book is not just a repository of knowledge; it's a starting point, an invitation to continue exploring the vast, uncharted territories of your dreams.

I urge you to see your dreams as fellow travellers on your life's journey, offering insights and lessons along the way. Keep a dream journal, engage with your dreams, and let them guide you towards deeper self-understanding and growth. Remember, every dream, whether puzzling, thrilling, or mundane, is a step towards understanding the complex narrative of your life.

I encourage you to embrace your dreams with curiosity and openness. Let them be your teachers, showing you aspects of yourself you might not recognize in your waking life. Dreams can be a source of healing, a catalyst for creativity, and a bridge to greater empathy and understanding of others.

Remember, the journey into the world of dreams doesn't end with the last word of this book. It continues every night in the quiet solitude of your mind. Countless dreams are still to be dreamt, interpreted, and learned from. The insights you gain from them can illuminate your waking life, offering clarity and direction.

As you progress, carry the knowledge and perspectives you've gained here. Let them inform your understanding of your dreams, but also remain open to the unique and personal messages your dreams have for you. Trust in the wisdom of your subconscious, for it speaks a language that is yours alone.

And so, dear dreamer, as you turn the final page of this book, know that your journey into the subconscious is an ever-unfolding story rich with mystery, beauty, and discovery. May your dreams be your compass, guiding you towards deeper self-awareness and fulfilment.

In gratitude and with the hope of endless enlightening dreams!

Glossary Of Terms

Understanding the world of dreams involves familiarizing oneself with various terms and concepts frequently used in dream analysis and interpretation. This glossary aims to provide clear definitions for some key terms in studying dreams.

Archetype: A universally recognized symbol or character that appears in all cultures' myths, stories, and dreams. Archetypes, a concept introduced by Carl Jung, represent fundamental human motifs of our experience as they shape our understanding and response to the world.

Collective Unconscious: A term coined by Carl Jung, referring to the part of the unconscious mind that a society, a people, or all humanity share. It contains the archetypes and is the repository of human knowledge and experience passed down through generations.

Conscious Mind: The aspect of the mind that is aware of one's surroundings, thoughts, and feelings. It is where we process our waking, logical, and rational experiences.

Dream Analysis: The method of uncovering the underlying meaning of dreams by interpreting the symbols, narratives, and emotions present in the dream content.

Dream Journal: A personal record where individuals can document their dreams. Keeping a dream journal helps in remembering and interpreting dreams more effectively.

Lucid Dreaming: A type of dream where the dreamer becomes aware that they are dreaming and, in some cases, can exert control over the dream characters, narrative, and environment.

Manifest Content: In Freudian dream analysis, this refers to the literal storyline and images of a dream, as opposed to the hidden psychological meaning of the dream (latent content).

Nightmares: Disturbing dreams that cause the dreamer to wake up feeling anxious, afraid, or distressed. Nightmares are often reflective of stress or anxiety in a person's waking life.

REM Sleep: Rapid Eye Movement sleep is a phase of sleep characterized by rapid movement of the eyes. REM sleep is typically when the most vivid dreaming occurs.

Subconscious Mind: The part of the mind that is not in current awareness but can influence thoughts and behaviour. Dreams are often seen as a window into the subconscious.

Symbolism: Using symbols in dreams to represent deeper meanings or concepts. Dream symbolism can vary widely between different cultures and individual experiences.

Unconscious Mind: The deepest part of the mind, which contains instincts, repressed memories, and desires. It is often explored in psychoanalytic theories of dreaming.

Latent Content: A term used in Freudian psychoanalysis

referring to the hidden psychological meaning of a dream, as opposed to the manifest content, which is the dream's literal storyline and imagery. The latent content often relates to repressed desires and thoughts.

Oneirology: The scientific study of dreams. This field encompasses the research and analysis of the process of dreaming, including the neurological mechanisms involved and the interpretation of dream content.

Premonitory Dreams: Dreams that are believed to predict or foresee future events. While often associated with supernatural beliefs, some psychological theories explore that premonitory dreams may subconsciously process subtle cues about the world that are not consciously noticed.

Sleep Paralysis: A phenomenon occurring either upon falling asleep or waking up, where an individual is conscious but unable to move or speak. During sleep paralysis, the person may experience vivid hallucinations, often leading to fear and confusion.

Sleep Cycle: The progression through different stages of sleep, typically including non-REM and REM stages. An average sleep cycle lasts about 90 minutes, and each stage of sleep plays a role in the body's restorative processes, including dreaming.

Symbolic Language: The language of symbols used in dreams to convey messages from the subconscious or unconscious mind. This language often requires interpretation to understand its meaning, as it uses images and symbolic scenarios rather than literal ones.

Theta Waves: Brainwave activity is associated with the early stages of sleep and some stages of wakefulness. Theta waves are often linked with creativity, meditation, and, in some stages of sleep, dreaming.

Vivid Dreams: Dreams that are particularly clear, intense, and memorable. These dreams are often recalled in great detail and can be more emotionally charged than typical dreams.

Waking Life: A term used to describe being awake, as opposed to being in the dream state. Events and experiences from one's waking life often influence the content and nature of dreams.

Resources For Further Reading

Resources for Further Reading

As our journey through "Dream Pilgrims - A Journey into the Subconscious" comes to a close, you may yearn to explore further into the captivating world of dreams. To assist in this quest, I've compiled a list of resources that offer additional insights and deepen your understanding of dreams. These resources include books, scientific studies, websites, and journals that are instrumental in dream research and interpretation.

Books

1. The Interpretation of Dreams by Sigmund Freud - A foundational text in the field of psychoanalysis, offering a detailed theory of the function and interpretation of dreams.

2. Man and His Symbols by Carl Jung- This book introduces the concept of the collective unconscious and the significance of symbols in dreams.

3. The Art of Dreaming by Carlos Castaneda - A fascinating exploration of the world of dreaming from a shamanic perspective.

4. Dreams by C.G. Jung- A collection of Jung's work that delves into the nature of dreaming, the interpretation of dreams, and their significance in psychological development.

5. Where People Fly and Water Runs Uphill by Jeremy Taylor - A book that uses dream analysis to explore personal growth and spiritual development.

Scientific Journals and Articles

1. Journal of Dream Research - An academic journal publishing original research articles on all aspects of dreaming.

2. Dreaming (American Psychological Association) - A journal that presents research findings related to dreams from a variety of disciplines.

3. International Journal of Dream Research - An open-access, peer-reviewed journal with a focus on dream research and its application.

Websites and Online Resources

1. The International Association for the Study of Dreams (IASD) - www.asdreams.org A leading organization for dream research, offering resources, conferences, and publications on dreaming.

2. **DreamsCloud** - www.dreamscloud.com A comprehensive resource for understanding and interpreting dreams, with a large database of dream symbols.

3. **The** **Lucidity** **Institute** - www.lucidity.com A resource dedicated to the research and advancement of lucid dreaming.

Online Courses and Workshops

1. Exploring the World of Lucid Dreaming - An online course based on the work of Stephen LaBerge, a pioneer in lucid dream research.

2. Jungian Dream Interpretation Online Course - A course offering insights into Carl Jung's method of dream analysis.

Podcasts and Video Series
1. The Dream Show with Michael Lennox - A podcast exploring all aspects of dreams and their interpretation.
2. In Your Dreams - A podcast series where hosts analyze and discuss various dreams submitted by listeners.

This collection of resources will provide you with diverse perspectives and deeper insights into the world of dreams. Whether you are a novice dream explorer or a seasoned dream interpreter, these resources will help you continue your journey into the fascinating exploration of the subconscious mind.

Happy dreaming!
Ranjeet Singh